IPHONE 12 USER GUIDE FOR SENIORS

**EASILY MASTER THE LATEST VERSION
OF YOUR IPHONE
THANKS TO STEP-BY-STEP TUTORIALS,
LARGE TEXTS, AND ILLUSTRATIONS.**

YOU WON'T FEEL IN DENIAL ANYMORE!

By: *BRANDON BALLARD*

Table of Content

Chapter 4: What's New in iOS 14

Chapter 5: How to Use the Internet and How to Activate the Connection

Chapter 6: How to Move Data from Android to Your iPhone

Chapter 7: Adding a Contact to Your Device

Chapter 8: Managing Calls

Chapter 9: Customize Messages

Chapter 10: Sync iPhone 12 with Computer

Chapter 11: Turn on iCloud backup

Chapter 17: Screenshots 109

Chapter 18: Apple services (Apple Card, Apple Music, Apple iCloud, Apple TV...) 112

Chapter 19: How to Activate Siri 122

Introduction

Are you just starting out on your new iPhone 12 and wondering how to set it up? We've got everything you need to remember.

There are a few steps you have to take to set up and start using your iPhone, whether you have just got a brand new iPhone 12 or iPhone 12 Pro, or an older version of Apple's famous phone.

The iPhone 12 is new for 2020. It was launched by Apple on October 13th. It features a 6.1-inch display, a new design, and weighs around 164 grams. It has an aluminum frame and a less rounded edge than recent iPhones. The rear is also made of glass. It's a dual sim phone that supports a Nano-SIM and an eSIM. It's a fully 5G capable phone and offers the broadest coverage worldwide.

The colors are blue, red, green, black and white. The iPhone 12 however doesn't come with a power adapter but it comes with the USB-C-to Lightning cable for charging and ear pods as part of Apple's drive to reduce carbon emissions and enable smaller and lighter packaging.

This manual completely simplified all the steps with clear pictures; screenshots, easy-to-understand tips, and tricks to solve every problem.

There are a lot more tips you will learn to ease the use of your iPhone. The iPhone is more loaded with many amazing features on iOS 14 that make life lovely and fulfilling.

As a beginner or a senior iPhone User, be rest assure that everything you need to know about your newly purchased iPhone 12, Mini, Pro, and Max

Will be clearly discussed below step by step without missing out on any important facts.

Also, note that the four of them have the same method of operational activities because they are all using the same iOS 14 that determines their functions and general beneficial features. Without further ado let's get started.

Chapter 1: Features of iPhone 12 Series

About the Special Body Structures

The iPhone 12, Mini, Pro, and Max body shapes are slightly redesigned to be more portable, attractive, and durable in preventing edges from cracking when fall.

Manufactured Color

- The iPhone 12 Mini and iPhone 12 come in black, white, red, green, and blue body appearances.
- The iPhone 12 Pro and Pro Max come in silver, graphite, gold, and pacific blue body appearances.

IP68 Waterproof and Dustproof Certification

The four iPhones could endure a maximum depth of 6 meters of water for approximately 30 minutes.

The iPhone Weight

- The iPhone 12 Mini—135 grams (4.76 ounces).
- The iPhone 12 weighs—164 grams (5.78 ounces).

- The iPhone 12 Pro weighs—189 grams (6.66 ounces).
- The iPhone 12 Pro Max weighs—228 grams (8.03 ounces).

General Screen Display

Screen diagonal size:

- The iPhone 12 Mini comes with 5.4 inches of Super Retina Extreme Dynamic Range (XDR) Screen Diagonal.
- The iPhone 12 & 12 Pro comes with 6.1 inches Super Retina XDR Screen Diagonal.
- The iPhone 12 Pro Max comes with 6.7 inches Super Retina XDR Screen Diagonal.

Height & Breadth

- The iPhone 12 Mini comes with 13.15cm (5.18 Inches) x 6.42cm (2.53 Inches).
- The iPhone 12 comes with 14.67cm (5.78 Inches) x 7.15cm (2.82 Inches).
- The iPhone 12 Pro come with 14.67cm (5.78 Inches) x 7.15cm (2.82 Inches).
- The iPhone 12 Pro Max 16.08cm (6.33 Inches) x 7.81cm (3.07 Inches).

iPhone 12

Height: 5.78 inches

Width: 2.82 inches

Depth: 0.29 inch

Weight: 5.78 ounces

The four iPhones have a Contrast Ratio of 2,000,000:1 of Organic Light Emitted Diode (OLED).

The iPhone 12 and 12 Pro is heavier than the iPhone 11 because the frame is made up of steel stainless while the iPhone 12 Mini and 12 are made up of the aluminum frame.

The iPhone 12, Mini, Pro & Max have a Ceramic Shield Glass to endure four-time protection of the iPhones from damage when they fall unconsciously.

They all have True Tone Display, P3 Wide Color Display, and Hepatic Touch.

Brightness Strength

- The iPhone 12 and Mini typically have 625nits maximum brightness while the iPhone 12 Pro and Pro Max have 800nits maximum brightness.
- They are all having the same Maximum Brightness of 1200nits High Dynamic Range (HDR).
- The iPhone 12 Mini has an HDR display of 2340 by 1080 pixel resolution at 476 pixels per inch (PPI).
- The iPhone 12 & Pro has an HDR display of 2532 by 1170 pixel resolution at 460ppi.
- The iPhone Pro Max has an HDR display of 2778 by 1284 pixel resolution at 458ppi.

A14 Bionic Support 5G Network Technology

The A14 Bionic has a capacity of 11.8 billion transistors with the highest speed of the Central Processing Unit (CPU), Graphics Processing Unit (GPU), and 80.37% Superfast Natural Engine.

All four iPhones could be used with 5G SIM which is the current fastest communication network service technology of this period.

This enables the mega-high speed of downloading and uploading with high-quality streaming activities on your iPhone.

A14 Bionic also improves maximum efficiency of transferring data, and network connectivity (No network interruption or Failure by the iPhone except the service provider).

Memory Storage

- The iPhone 12 and Mini: Both iPhones come with these various capacities of 64GB, 128GB, and 256GB. The higher the memory capacity in the iPhone, the higher the price of the iPhone because the storage size of the memory determines the cost of the iPhone.
- The iPhone 12 Pro and Max: Both iPhones come with these various capacities of 128GB, 256GB, and 512GB.

Rear (Back) Cameras

- The iPhone 12 and Mini cameras: The iPhone 12 and Mini rear cameras comprises dual camera of Ultra Wide and Wide Camera. The 12MP Ultra Wide Camera can cover 1200 Field View with the help of a 5-Element Lens, f/2.4 Aperture, and 13mm Focal Length. The 12MP Wide Camera has absolute Focus Pixels, stabilized optical imageability with the aid of sensor-shift, 7-elements of f/1.6 Aperture, and 26mm Focal Length. Video Version: They have Dolby Vision HDR video with the ability to record approximately 30 fps. Zoom Magnification: The iPhone 12 and Max have an optical zoom range of four times (4x)
- The iPhone 12 Pro and Max Cameras: They have three different 12MP Cameras that include Ultra Wide, Wide, and Telephoto Cameras. The 12MP Camera uses a 5-element lens with a 13mm focal length to cover a 1200 field of view with an f/2.4 aperture. The 12MP Wide Camera has an absolute Focus Pixel, Stabilizing Optical Image with the help of sensor-shift, 7-Elements Lens of 26mm Focal Length with unto 27 percent improved low light ca-

pacity. The 12MP Telephoto Camera uses a 6-element lens with a distance capacity of 52mm focal length, stabilizing optical image, 4 times optical zoom range, and f/2.0 Aperture. Zoom Magnification: The iPhone 12 Pro has an optical zoom range of four times (4x) while iPhone 12 Pro Max has a capacity of the optical zoom range of six times (6x). Apple ProRAW: This is designed for an iPhone user using a professional camera to take massive raw images; provides a large file to save the collective Raw images on your iPhone. It will also enable you to edit your images and save them as JPEG documents. It adds different color effects on the image during raw image display. It also has a Light Detection and Ranging (LiDAR) Scanner for Night Mode Portrait, rapid autofocus in poor light to produce distinct background and cop-out the real images, and carry-out next stage of Augmented Reality (AR). It could be used to rearrange the position of the images on your portrait coverage. When press and hold any farther image, move it close to the other image(s) to remove in-between distance.

Video Recording Capacity

The iPhone 12, Mini, Pro & Max

- They have 4K Video recording at 24 frames per second (fps), 30 fps, or 60 fps.
- They have 1080p HD Video recording capacity that could record at 30 fps or 60 fps.
- The high dynamic range (HDR) could record with Dolby Vision at approximately 30 fps.
- They have an extended dynamic range that could record approximately 60 fps.

- They are all having Video Optical Image & Time-lapse stabilization.

Zoom Magnification

- The iPhone 12 & Mini have optical zoom out of times two and times three of digital zoom up.
- The iPhone 12 Pro has optical zoom out & in of times two and times six of digital zoom up.
- The iPhone 12 Pro Max has optical zoom out of time two and a half, and zoon in times two with times seven digital zoom up.
- They all have a QuickTake Video feature.
- They all have Slo-Mo (Slow Motion) Video of 1080p at the rate of 120 fps or 240 fps.
- They are all having Audio and Stereo recording features

Front-Facing Camera

The iPhone 12, Mini, Pro, and Max

- The four smartphones have super-quality of 12 Megapixel (MP) image productions, TrueDepth Camera with f/2.2 Aperture.
- The Photos have Smart HDR 3, Portrait mode with advanced Bokeh and Depth Control.
- They have 4K, 1080p, and 720p of cinematic video stabilizing capacity.
- 4K Video recording at the rate of 24 fps, 30 fps, or 60 fps.
- However, the front-facing camera has the same functions and capabilities as rear cameras. It is one of the outstanding improvements in the current iPhone 12 Mini, 12, 12 Pro, and 12 Pro Max that have the same number of Megapixels of Rear and Front Facing Camera. Therefore, you could completely perform

everything you could do with the rear cameras.

The Lighting Feature Effects

They all have six distinct lighting effects to beautify your photos.

MagSafe Charger & Wireless Charger

It is a magnetic charger that quickly charges the iPhone with the help of the in-built magnetic components at the back of the iPhone that sends electric charge into the iPhone charging coil which in turn transfers power to the battery.

Connection

1. Get or Buy Apple 20Watt (W) USB-C Power Adapter or other acceptable power adapter and connect the MagSafe Charger which is not coming with the iPhone 12.
2. Remove the Wireless Charger from its wallet.
3. Put the MagSafe Charger at the center back of the iPhone. If you are using MagSafe Case position the charger inside the designed face at the back.
4. Let your iPhone face up.
5. In a second, a circular green will show on the iPhone screen to indicate the charging level.

Battery Capacity

- The iPhone 12 Mini comes with a battery size of 2227mAh.
- The iPhone 12 and Pro come with a battery size of 2815mAh.
- The iPhone 12 Pro Max comes with a battery size 3687mAh.
- The iPhone 12, Mini, Pro, and Max have rechargeable built-in Lithium-ion batteries with an hour different power capacity.

- The iPhone 12 and Pro have two hours more power capacity than iPhone 12 Mini, while the iPhone 12 Pro Max has five hours more power capacity than iPhone 12 Mini.

Streamed Audio & Video Playback

- The iPhone 12 Mini can stream playback audio sound for closely 50 hours and stream playback video for 10 hours.
- The iPhone 12 and Pro have the same ability to stream playback audio for 65 hours and video for 11 hours.
- The iPhone 12 Max has more ability to stream playback audio for 80 hours and video could last up to 12 hours.

Charging Duration

The four iPhones could be approximately charged up to 50% within 30minutes when you use Apple 20W USB-C Power Adapter or other compatible higher adapter recommended.

You could get the original and reliable power adapter on Amazon.com or Verizon.com.

Components of the iPhone 12, Mini, Pro, and Max Notch

The Notch location is the top black center of your iPhone where there is a Face Sensor, Stereo Speaker with Microphone, and Front-Facing Camera.

- Face Sensor: This recognizes the original owner's face that has been captured and saved for Face ID during setup or later performed in the Settings. The sensor will be displaying blinking infrared light to scan your face for the lock screen of your iPhone to be unlocked.

- **Stereo Speaker with In-Build Microphone:** This will enable you to hear the audible sound and send voice sound to anyone calling you. It also helps during live-voice recording.
- **Front-Facing Camera:** The camera comes with more improved megapixels of 12 and is designed to capture every image or object at the front of your iPhone screen including moving objects or living things like animals, plants, and humans. Therefore, you can use the Front-Facing Camera to take a personal picture called a "selfie" directly without asking for any external support.

As is customary for an iPhone, nothing much should be expected in terms of box contents. The relatively slender box which is predominantly white for the regular iPhone 12 and black for the iPhone 12 Pro contains the phone itself, a USB type C cable, a sim tool, and an apple sticker. You would have to get yourself an adapter and/or a MagSafe charger for wireless charging.

Battery Life

It seems that Apple is continuing its trend to make sure that the standard iPhone has good longevity, and the iPhone 12 is experiencing improvements in battery life, which means less travel for the charger.

Apple has unmistakably accomplished some work here to ensure things are not really well horrendous with regards to power management. With the iPhone 12, it is said that it lasted well enough on a full charge, in particular, compared to iPhones from a few years ago. That said, there is no other leap forward in battery life - it is comparable to the iPhone 11 at best, and perhaps a little worse.

Chapter 2: How to Turn on/off iPhone

How Do You Switch On the iPhone 12 and 12 Pro

Select and hold the side button.

How to Sleep or Wake Your iPhone 12 and 12 Pro

Click on the side button.

How to Turn Off Your iPhone 12 and 12 Pro

1. Press and hold the side button + either volume buttons.

2. Slide to turn off.

Turn on iPhone 12

1. Press and hold the side button or the sleep/wake button (depending on your model) until the Apple logo appears.
2. If the iPhone is not activated, you may need to charge the battery.
3. Do one of the following:
   - Touch Configure manually, follow the instructions on the screen.
   - If you have another iPhone, iPad, or iPod touch with iOS 11, iPadOS 13, or later, you can use Quick Launch to set up your

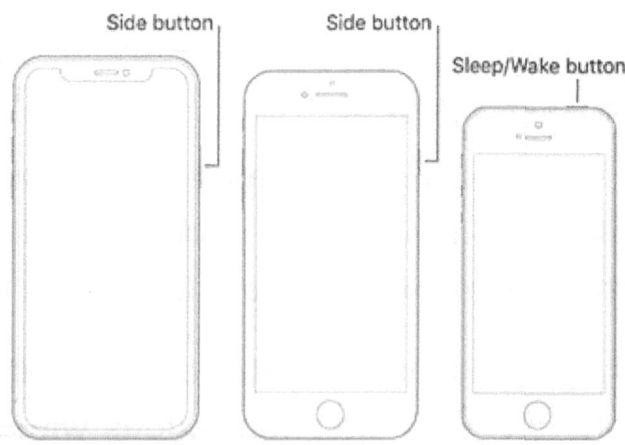

new device automatically. Put the two devices together; follow the onscreen instructions to safely copy many of your iCloud settings, preferences, and keychain. At that point, you can reestablish the remainder of your information and substance on your new gadget from your iCloud reinforcement. Or, if both devices are running iOS 12.4, iPadOS 13, or later, you can transfer all your data wirelessly from your old device to your new one. Keep your devices together and keep them in place until the migration process is complete. You can also transfer your data with a wired connection between your devices.

- If you are blind or visually impaired, double-click the side button (on an iPhone with Face ID) or triple-click the Home button (on other iPhone models) to have VoiceOver turn on the screen reader. You can also double-tap the screen with 3 fingers.

Chapter 3: Set up the iPhone 12

Your brand new iPhone is ready for you to set up right out of the box. A nice "Hello" will welcome you. From this stage, you will be able to customize your iPhone as if it were new or move your data from another phone, like an Android or Windows phone. Do not worry; we will walk you through it all.

In one of three ways, you can set up your iPhone 12, start new, restore it from another iPhone, or import content from a non-Apple phone. In more depth, here's what each of those choices means.

Set as new means beginning everything from scratch, every environment. This is for people who have never before used a smartphone or online services or who want to feel completely brand new with their iPhone.

Restore from a previous iPhone, iPad, or iPod touch backup-This can be accomplished with iCloud online or iTunes or Finder (macOS Catalina) over USB. This is for those who have had a previous iOS device and are switching to a new one and want the new one intact with all they had on the older device.

Importing from Android, BlackBerry, or Windows Phone-To make Android simpler; Apple has a Google Play app, but online services allow you to transfer a lot of data from any old mobile. This is for individuals moving from a different mobile device to an iPhone or iPad.

The moment you turn your new iPhone on for the first time, in many languages, you will be greeted with "Hello." If you start from scratch, restore from a different iPhone, or turn from Android, it's the same.

1. To get started, touch the slide and slide your finger across the screen.

2. Your language is picked.

3. Select a country or region for you.

4. Select a network with Wi-Fi. You can choose to set up later if you are not in the Wi-Fi network range. Instead, pick Cellular. (More details on how to set up your iPhone with Wi-Fi will be discussed extensively later in the book) At this point, you can choose to set up your new iPhone with the same passcode and settings as another iPhone using Automatic Setup. If you want to manually set up your new iPhone, continue with the steps below.

5. After reading about the Data & Privacy details for Apple, tap Proceed.

6. Tap Allow Services for Venue. Select Skip Location Services if you don't want to allow localization services at this time. You can manually activate such location services, including Maps.

Inserting the Sim and Setting up Mobile Data Plan

A SIM is required to access Cellular and data services when connected to a GSM or CDMA network. The iPhone uses a na-no-SIM.

Certain functions and capabilities of the iPhone would not be functional until a wireless network is available. You may need to contact your preferred wireless service provider for more details regarding roaming, availability of access, restrictions, and policy governing the wireless service.

To Insert the Nano-SIM

1. Insert a SIM ejector pin into the hole of the SIM tray and push forward.
2. The SIM tray will pop-out and can be removed from the iPhone.
3. Put the SIM into the SIM tray in a way that it aligns with the shape of the SIM tray.
4. Place the tray back gently into the space from which it was ejected in the iPhone.

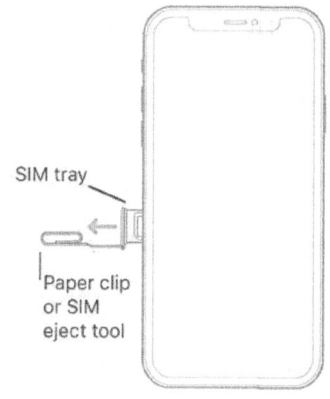

SIM tray

Paper clip
or SIM
eject tool

You can activate a mobile data plan on your iPhone including a roaming arrangement (depending on the network provider's policy). Do this by navigating to Settings > Mobile Data and follow the prompts.

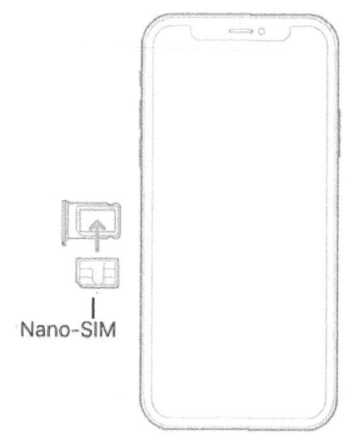

Nano-SIM

Set up Assistant

The setup assistant is auto-activated. The setup assistant was built as a walkthrough guide for the first steps required to use the iPhone. To select, click, double click and move items around on the screen, use the trackpad.

Choose your Country and click Continue. You can change this later by navigating to Settings > Language and Region.

Next, pick the Keyboard layout of your choice and click Continue. Choose your network type (Wi-Fi, Ethernet, or none and click continue). Select your preferred Internet Protocol (IP) from the connection type list and enter the IP address, subnet mask, default gateway, and DNS server address in the required fields and then click Continue. If there are available Wi-Fi networks available, just select your Wi-Fi network and enter the passcode to connect to the Internet through the network.

Apple's Data and Privacy Information come up on the screen. The information would help you understand how Apple makes use of the data it collects from you as you use the iPhone especially in terms of product improvement and research focused on future updates. Read through the information and click Continue.

To transfer information to this device, select the right option from the available options like iPhone, iPhone, iPhone touch, or Android device. If you do not have existing Data to transfer or would prefer to do this later, select the option Don't transfer any information now.

Enter your Apple ID in the required field, click Continue and input the corresponding password. If you do not already have one, you can create one during this set-up. After getting an Apple ID, you can then sign in to your device. The Apple ID is very important, and it comprises of an email address and a password. Just one Apple ID is required to use any Apple Service and it is best practice not to share the details with anyone. Apple ID is the account that will enable you to get the most out of your Apple devices—including downloading apps from the App Store, Siri, buying music and movies from iTunes Store, pushing and storing content in iCloud and other Apple resources.

If the password you entered is correct, you will be automatically signed into apps and services that require Apple ID. If you do not remember your Apple ID password, click on the 'Forgot Apple ID or password?' link that is available in the sign-in window for the recovery of the password.

The Terms and Conditions window contains license terms for using the Apple device that you need to read and click Agree.

Input all the compulsory fields and then click on Create a Computer Account window and then Continue. Congratulations! You have created a new user account with which you can log into your iPhone with admin rights allowing you to download and install apps, create other user accounts and make system changes.

Next, configure your device with frequently used settings by clicking Continue on the Express Setup window. This takes you to the Home Screen page and the setup is complete.

Sign in with Your Apple ID

1. If you did not log in during configuration, do the following:
2. Go to settings.
3. Tap Sign in to iPhone.
4. Enter your Apple ID and password.
5. If you do not have an Apple ID, you can create one.
6. To protect your account with 2-factor authentication, enter the six-digit verification code.
7. If you forget your Apple ID or password, see Recovering Your Apple ID Website.

Manage Apple ID and iCloud Settings on iPhone

An Apple ID is the account you use to access Apple services such as the App Store, iTunes Store, Apple Books, Apple Music, FaceTime, iCloud, iMessage, and more.

With iCloud, you can store photos, videos, documents, music, apps, and more securely—and keep them up to date on all your devices. With iCloud, you can easily share your photos, calendars, locations, and more with your friends and family. You can even use iCloud to locate your iPhone if you lose it.

iCloud provides a free email account and 5GB of storage for emails, documents, photos and videos, and backups. Purchased music, apps, TV shows, and books are not included in the available storage. You can update your iCloud storage directly from the iPhone.

Note: **Some iCloud features have minimum system requirements. The availability of iCloud and its services varies by country and region.**

Steps on How to Set up Face ID on Your iPhone 12

The Face ID setup is identical to the Touch ID setup, except simpler. As part of your initial iPhone setup, iOS will offer to let you set up a Face ID. But you can also set up Face ID whenever you like and reset it.

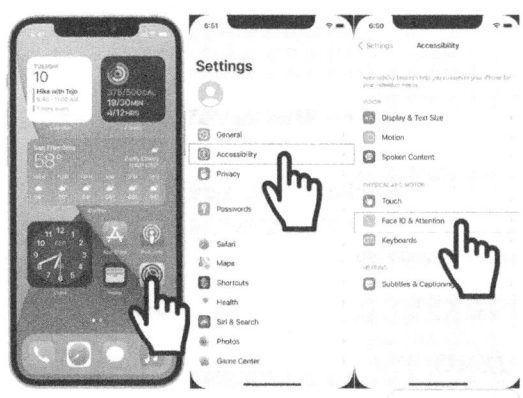

1. Press "Settings"

2.   Find "Face ID and passcode"

3.   Set Face ID

4.   Press start and follow the step-by-step instructions on the screen to set it up

5.   Press "Done". If you did not previously select an iPhone lock code, type in a code of your choice twice.

6.   Next to "iPhone Unlock" you can choose via the indicator whether to turn the feature on or off. Same for "iTunes & App Store."

7.   Slide your finger up from the bottom of the screen to return to the home screen.

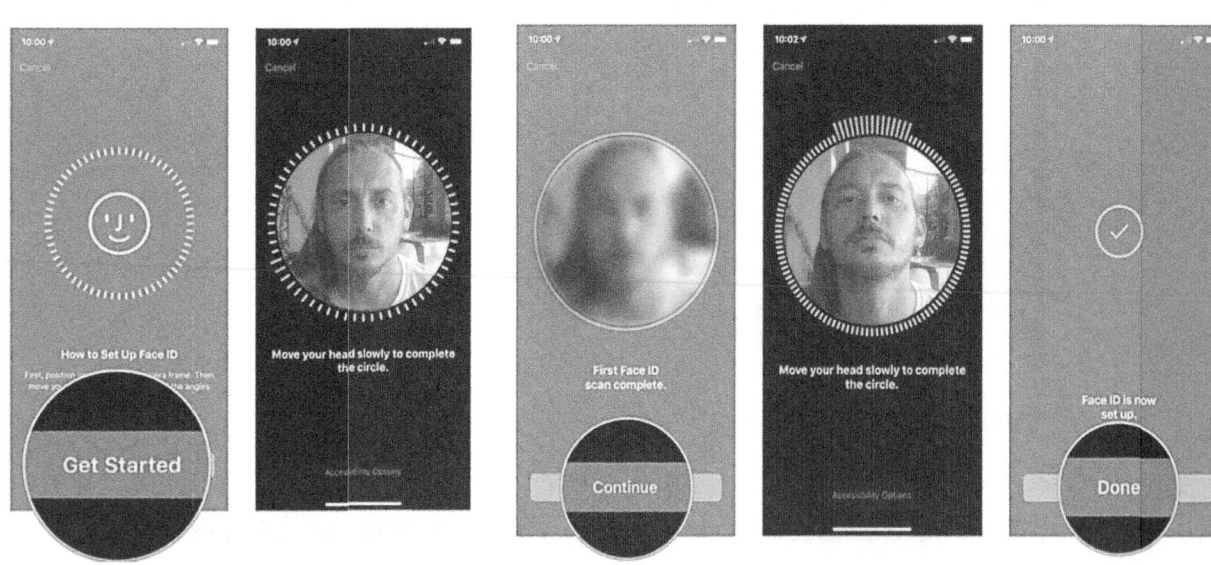

You can now begin to use Face ID on your new iPhone 12!

How Do You Turn off Require Attention for Face ID

By default, your iPhone with Face ID support will require you to look at it before it is authenticated. If you want to be able to unlock it without looking directly at your iPhone screen, you can turn it off for reasons of usability or convenience. It's not as safe, but you can do it if you want to

28

unlock your iPhone while it's on the table or if you're keeping it sideways.

Note: **In order to authenticate you, the Face ID device also needs to be able to see your eyes, nose, and mouth. But there's a limit to its field of view, even with the attention off.**

    1. Open Settings from your home screen.

    2. Click on the Passcode & Face ID.

    3. Input your passcode.

    4. Switch the required attention for Face ID to off

    5. Click OK when the security alert pops up.

    6. Click the switch again the second time if you need to Require Attention back on.

How to Reset Face ID

If you want to change the face of the person that is registered on your iPhone or you just want to redo your Face ID setup for whatever reason, you can!

Note: **No confirmation is needed; dear Apple, add a confirmation dialog, please! So your face ID will be gone the moment you press the button, and you'll have to set it up again to get it back.**

    1. From your home screen, open settings.

    2. Click the Passcode & Face ID.

    3. Input your passcode.

    4. Click Face ID Reset.

Change Your Apple ID Settings

Go to Settings> [your name].

Do one of the following:

1. Update your contact information.
2. Change your password.
3. Manage Family Sharing.

Know Your Settings

These are some of the various settings you can modify on your iPhone 12 to improve its responsiveness and the overall user experience. There are several settings in your iPhone 12, so it helps to play around with your device a little until you get used to it. This is a brief overview to show you some of the possible things with your new iPhone, but there's a lot more about your device you can figure out on your own.

Personal Information

Right at the top of the settings screen, you will see your name along with your Apple ID. If you tap on that, you will be able to reset your Apple ID and change some things about your iCloud and iTunes accounts.

Underneath your name, there's the Airplane Mode, Wi-Fi, Bluetooth, and Cellular. These are all features you can access from the Control Center, which you can open by swiping downwards from your screen's top right corner.

Notifications Settings

Right below this panel are the notifications. If you tap the notifications settings open, you will see the Show Previous option, which controls when and how notifications are displayed. If you tap on the Show Previous option, you will see three choices to pick from: Always, When Unlocked, and Never. If you select Show Previous Always, you will always see previous notifications on the Lock Screen. If you choose Show Previous When Unlocked, no notification will be displayed until your iPhone is unlocked. Finally, if you select the Show Previous Never option, then your device will not display notifications whether it is locked or unlocked. As a recommendation, choose the "Show Previous When Unlocked" option, as one will have to unlock your iPhone before they can view your notifications.

Do Not Disturb settings

The Do Not Disturb settings in the Settings app control all the Do Not Disturb feature configurations, which helps to put your device in silent mode when you don't want interference caused by incoming calls, messages, and other notification sounds. In the Do Not Disturb settings screen within the Settings app, you can also schedule when the feature becomes active and when it comes off automatically. For instance, you can schedule the Do Not Disturb feature to become active at 10 PM during bedtime and turn it off by 7 AM.

General settings

You can update your operating system (OS) from the General settings in the Settings app. To do this, tap on General in the settings app, and then tap on Software Update.

There are a few additional options in the General settings screen that may be helpful. Down the general settings screen is the iPhone storage. This contains vital information about how much storage space all the different apps in your iPhone are taking up. It also gives you the option of getting rid of any app you feel is not useful but is consuming a sizable amount of your storage space.

You can also customize the keyboard and set usage restrictions for specific files and applications from the general settings.

Display & Brightness settings

Just below General in the settings app is the Display & Brightness settings. In this settings screen, you can adjust your display's brightness, modify the size of the texts shown on your display, decide how long your display should stay on without activity before auto-locking, etc.

Sounds and Haptics

The Sounds and Haptics settings allow you to change your phone sounds (ringtones, message tones, etc.), while Haptics deals with your iPhone's vibration behavior.

Check for Software Updates

Once the setup is completed, go to the Home screen and click on App Store. Select Find and install any software updates to find out and install any available software updates. You can begin to use your iPhone once your software is up to date.

How to Plug in the Power Adapter, Connect the Cables and Charge the Device

Remove the film material around the power adapter. The film is intended as a protective cover around the adapter to prevent it from damage.

Next, the AC plug with the USB cable fixed into it should be inserted into a power outlet and the other end of the cable should be inserted into the power adapter port of the iPhone. (Ensure the power ratings of the plug and the power outlet are compatible to avoid damaging the device).

You can also charge the iPhone wirelessly with a Qi-certified charger (available as an accessory at Apple stores).

Connect the charger to a power source and place the iPhone on the charger face up and wait for a few seconds for it to start charging. For s smooth experience, remove any casings from the iPhone and ensure that there is no barrier between it and the Qi-certified charger. The iPhone models that support wireless charging are iPhone 8, iPhone 8 Plus, iPhone X, iPhone XS, iPhone XS Max, iPhone XR, iPhone Pro Max, iPhone Pro, iPhone SE (second generation), iPhone 11, iPhone 12, iPhone 12 mini, iPhone 12 Pro and iPhone 12 Pro Max.

The iPhone is fitted with a lithium-ion rechargeable battery that is lighter, charges faster, and has a long life.

It is important to ensure the device is charging so that it does not shut down unexpectedly or run out of battery during the setup process.

The battery charge status icon at the top right corner of the screen indicates the battery level and charging status. A battery charging icon shows that the device is well connected to the AC source. The battery charges faster when the device is off or in a sleep mode. Once the battery is fully charged, please remove the cable and disconnect the AC plug from the power outlet.

For optimal usage of the battery and to conserve the battery power, disconnect any accessories connected to the iPhone that are not in use, reduce the display brightness and close any unused apps.

Access Reachability Mode

You will have to set it up first, unlike the other gestures.

1. From the home screen, open Settings.

2. Just tap General.

3. On Usability, click it.

4. Toggle on the Reachability.

Once set up:

1. Touch the gesture area at the very bottom of the iPhone 12 screen with your finger.

2. Swipe down.

From the top right of Reachability, you can also swipe to access the Control Center.

Put iPhone In Ringtone or Silent Mode

Toggle the ring/mute switch to put iPhone to ring mode or silent mode.

In-ring mode, iPhone plays all sounds. In silent mode (the switch is shown in orange), the iPhone won't ring or play alerts or other sound effects (but the iPhone may still vibrate).

Set Sound and Vibration Options

1. Go to Settings> Sounds and Touches (on supported models) or Sounds (on other iPhone models).
2. Drag the slider under Ringtones and alerts to adjust the volume for all sounds.
3. Touch a sound type, such as ringtone or text tone, to set the tones and vibration patterns for sounds.
4. Do any of the following:
   - Choose a tone. Ringtones are played for approaching calls,

clock cautions, and clock; Text tones are utilized for instant messages, new voice messages, and different alarms.

- Tap Vibrate, then choose a vibration pattern, or tap Create new vibration to create your own.

Enable or Disable Haptic Feedback

1. Go to Settings> Sounds and Touches on supported models.
2. Enable or turn on the system's haptic technology.

With System Haptics off, you won't hear or feel vibrations from incoming calls and alerts.

Find Settings on iPhone

1. Tap Settings on the Home screen (or app library).
2. Scroll down to reveal the search field, enter a term such as "iCloud," and then tap a setting.

How to Move Data from Old to New iPhone

If you did not transfer files from your old device during configuration, do the following:

Step 1:

1. Download and install Anytrans on the computer.
2. Open it and connect the iPhones to the computer using USB cables.
3. Choose the "Phone Switcher."
4. Click on "Phone to iPhone" mode.

Step 2:

1. Choose the device from which the info is to be transferred and

place it in the new device

2. Click the "Next" button to continue. It helps you transfer data from Android and iPhone to your new iPhone at the same time.

Step 3:

1. Select file categories to transfer.
2. Click "Next" button to move data from the old iPhone to the new iPhone.

Tips: Besides, you can also go to the category management screen to preview first and then select the data you want to transfer.

Wake and Unlock iPhone

The iPhone turns off the screen to save power, locks itself for security, and goes to sleep when you're not using it. You can quickly wake up and unlock your iPhone when you want to use it again. The iPhone will lock automatically if you don't touch the screen for about a minute.

Wake up iPhone

Do one of the following to activate iPhone:

- Touch the side button or the sleep/sleep button.
- Pick up the iPhone. You can turn off Raise to turn on in Settings> Display & brightness.
- Touch the screen

Unlock iPhone with Face ID

1. Touch the screen or lift the iPhone to wake it up, and then glance at your iPhone.
2. The lock symbol moves from off to open (unlock) to show that

the iPhone is opened.

3. Slide up from the base (bottom) of the screen.

4. Press the side button to re-lock iPhone. iPhone locks automatically if you don't touch the screen for about a minute.

Unlock iPhone with Touch ID

1. On an iPhone with a home button, press the home button with your finger that you enrolled with Touch ID.

2. Press the side button or the sleep/wake button (depending on your model) to re-lock iPhone. iPhone locks automatically if you don't touch the screen for about a minute.

Unlock iPhone with a Password

1. Slide up from the base (bottom) of the lock screen (on an iPhone with Face ID) or tap down the Home button (on other iPhone models).

2. Enter the passcode (if you have set the iPhone to require a passcode).

3. Press the side button or sleep/wake button (depending on your model) to re-lock iPhone. iPhone locks automatically if you don't touch the screen for about a minute.

Change iPhone's Language

With the iPhone 12, users can access the Apple application store to purchase various games, utilities, and ringtones.

Some users who speak other languages may have difficulty finding their way through the app store as the default language is English.

However, users can change the language to one that they are comfortable with.

1. Go to "Settings" on your device.
2. You'll see the icon that appears like two gears moving together.
3. Tap "Settings," which is first in the third menu down.
4. Scroll down until you see the "International" option and click on it.
5. Tap the "Language" option located on the International menu. Choose your desired language. A check will appear close to the language you chose.
6. Press the "Home" button to return to the home screen. When you open the app store, the new language will appear.

How to Customize VoiceOver

Voiceover can recognize a lot of different things on display now. It uses on-device intelligence to recognize elements on your screen to improve overall support.

1. Go to VoiceOver Recognition
2. Turn ON (or OFF) Image Descriptions and Screen Recognition
3. Turning ON Image Description and Screen Recognition allows your phone to explain anything you tap on and things on your display. Screen recognition will detect everything from interface controls to aid in navigating apps.

How to Adjust Volume

You can adjust the ringer volume on your iPhone via Settings or the volume button on the side of your device.

Via Settings

1. Head to settings, then go to "Sounds and Haptics."
2. Drag the slider under "Ringer and Alerts" to adjust the volume level.

Via Volume Buttons

1. First, go to settings, then go to "Sounds & Haptics."
2. Scroll to ringer and alerts, turn on "Change with Buttons."

If you enable this feature, the volume buttons will now have two functions:

- Ringer and alerts function when you are not using media.
- Controls media volume when watching a video or listening to music.

An Unresponsive Phone

If your phone is totally unresponsive, don't panic. Quickly tap the volume up button, then the volume down button, then press and hold the side power button until the Apple logo appears.

How to Turn the Device Off and On Again

Simultaneously hold down the volume up button and the side buttons for few seconds.

Slide the onscreen power symbol to the right.

Hold the side button until the Apple logo appears to turn it back on.

This method carries out a graceful shutdown followed by the usual turn-on process. I recommend trying to use this method to solve the issue first.

How to Force Restart

Quickly press and release the volume up button, followed by the volume down button.

Hold down the side button and release it when the Apple logo appears.

Although this method will try to restart your device, the issue might not actually be resolved. If the iPhone does not turn back on, Apple's support pages give more tips, including how to recover the device in more serious cases.

Note: When restarting your device, make sure to pay attention and follow all instructions properly. Specifically the case if you confuse the two instructions and end up holding down the up volume and side buttons for a long time. In doing so, the Emergency SOS feature will begin a five-second countdown, where it will count down from five and vibrate with each number as the Emergency SOS slider fills up. If the counter gets to 0 and you are still holding both buttons down, your phone will consider the bar full and dial the emergency services, which may inform the police or an ambulance of your location. Just to pay attention and if the vibration and countdown begin, release the buttons.

How to Update iOS

1. Go to Settings, then to General, and tap on Software Update.
2. Tap "Download and Install."
3. Tap on Install to update. Or you can select Later and tap on Install Tonight or Remind Me Later. If you select Install Tonight, plug your device into power before you go to bed. Your device will automatically update overnight. Enter your passcode if you are asked to.

To turn automatic updates on:

1. Head to Settings, then to General, and then tap on Software Update

2. Customize "Automatic Updates," then turn on "Install iOS Updates."

How to Backup iPhone

You need a Wi-Fi connection for this.

Back up Apps

1. Go to Settings and tap your Apple ID. If prompted, sign in with your Apple ID.

2. Tap on iCloud and tap the slider next to the desired apps. Tap on the iCloud Backup app at the bottom of the list.

3. Turn on iCloud Backup and tap on Back Up. Wait for the backup to complete.

Back up Contacts

1. Go to Settings and tap on your Apple ID. Sign in if prompted.

2. Tap on iCloud and then switch on the Contacts slider. Select Merge contacts with iCloud if you are asked to.

3. Tap on the iCloud Backup app at the bottom. Turn on iCloud Backup and tap on Back Up.

4. Wait for the backup to complete.

Back up Media and Pictures from Phone

1. Go to Settings and tap on your Apple ID. Sign in if prompted.

2. Tap on iCloud and then tap Photos. Turn the iCloud Photo Library slider on.

3. Tap on iCloud to return to the previous screen. Next, tap the

iCloud Backup app.

4. Turn on iCloud Backup and tap on Back Up.
5. Wait for the backup to complete.

How to restore iPhone 12 to Default

A master reset restores your phone's default settings and may delete files on your internal storage.

- Back up all your data on the internal memory.
- If you enabled Apple FMiP Activation Lock, you need to access the internet to complete these steps.
- Head to settings, then to general, and then select Reset.

Select from any of the options:

- **Reset All Settings:** Use this option before you attempt a master reset.
- **Erase All Content and Settings:** Use this option for master reset. Make sure you select Erase all and keep plans.
- **Reset Network Settings:** This will erase any saved Wi-Fi profiles.
- **Reset Keyboard Dictionary**
- **Reset Home Screen Layout**
- **Reset Location and Privacy**
- Enter your password if you are asked to.
- Confirm your selection.

How to Restore All Contents from Backup

Option 1:

Erase all current data. You can restore all your data if you backed them up via iTunes. if you do a restore with iTunes, all your current data will be erased. Use the following steps:

1. On your computer, open iTunes. Connect your phone to the computer and enter your passcode if you are asked to or select "Trust this Computer."
2. Select the device in iTunes or the Finder window to continue.
3. Click on "Select Backup" and then depending on the date, select the most relevant backup.
4. Click on "Restore."

Option 2:

Do not need to erase data (Recommend). If you don't want to remove all your current data, use PanFone Data Transfer to restore it.

1. Download and install PanFone on your computer. Launch the app.
2. Connect your device to the computer via a USB cable.
3. Click on the iTunes Backup File. Select "Restore" and click on "iTunes backup." If you have already synced your device with iTunes on the computer, then PanFone Data Transfer can detect the iTunes backup files. Click on "Next" to load iTunes backup from your computer.
4. Next, all saved iTunes backups will be enlisted. Select one backup according to its date or size. Then click Start.
5. Click on the Desired Contents from iTunes Backup. All data from the backup file will be available to restore. Just mark the ones you need then click "Next" to load the files. This might take a while depending on the size
6. Retrieve the Files from iTunes Backup to your device. Once the data is loaded, select the files you want to retrieve then click "Recover to Computer" or "Recover to iOS 14 device" as needed.

After the process is complete, your device will automatically reboot. Do not disconnect the device until the process is successful.

Chapter 4: What's New in iOS 14

iOS 14 is one of the biggest iOS updates to date by Apple, introducing changes to the home screen design, major new features, existing app updates, upgrades to Siri, and several other tweaks that streamline the iOS interface. iOS 14 is now available for use on all compatible devices, so you should see it in Settings at the Software Update section First off, iOS 14 offers a redesigned Home Screen that supports widgets for the first time. With a Picture in Picture mode, users can simultaneously watch videos or talk on FaceTime while also using other apps. Now, Siri is smarter and can answer a lot of questions with info pulled from the internet. Siri also sends audio messages. Keyboard dictation also runs on the device, offering a more privacy layer to the dictated messages.

iOS 14's new Home Screen allows for more customization with the incorporation of widgets, options to hide apps pages, and the new App Library that shows all your apps at a glance. Additional iOS 14 features include: Translate, home app, air pods, digital car keys, find my, safari, health, the weather app, and accessibility.

iPhone OS 14 is the newest operating system for the iPhone and is packed with so many useful features, bug fixes, and new capabilities that would make for an awesome update. The update is free just like previous Apple software updates.

iOS 14 Compatible Devices

The iOS 14 is also compatible with the following iPhone models:

- iPhone 12
- iPhone 12 mini
- iPhone 12 Pro
- iPhone 12 Pro Max
- iPhone 11
- iPhone Pro
- iPhone Pro Max
- iPhone XR
- iPhone XS
- iPhone XS Max
- iPhone X
- iPhone SE (1st and 2nd generation) iPhone 8
- iPhone 8 Plus
- iPhone 7
- iPhone 7 Plus
- iPhone 6s
- iPhone 6s Plus

How to Upgrade to iOS 14

Once you decide to upgrade to the new iOS 14 and device compatibility is confirmed, first back up your device. Afterward, navigate to Settings > General > Software Update and click on Automatic Updates. This will ensure that whenever an update is available, the iPhone will download and install the update at night provided the device is charging and connected to Wi-Fi.

You may also visit Settings > General > Software Update. Here, you will see the current version of the iOS your device is running on and the availability of an update.

You can also update using your Mac by connecting it to your iPhone with a USB cable.

In the Finders sidebar of your MacBook, click on your iPhone > General at the top of the window.

In the iTunes app of your Windows PC, click on the iPhone icon close to the top left-hand corner of the iTunes window and then on Summary.

Next, click Check for Update and if available, click on Update.

Changes and Improvements in the iOS 14

- Compact Calls View such that all incoming calls (both from FaceTime and 3rd Party apps) are visible in the compact Calls view. Better still, it does not take up the full screen.

- Newly redesigned Home Screen that allows you to see more information on the Widgets. You can choose from a variety of sizes, arrange them in any way you choose, or add a Smart Stack that can take factors like location, activity, and time into consideration for the Widget displays.
- App clips for specific tasks that can be accessed by using the camera to scan QR codes, and in Messages, Maps, and the Safari browser.
- App library on the Home Screen that makes it easy to organize and navigate through apps installed on the device.
- Translate app to become more in-tune with different languag-

es and have easy conversations (voice or text) in 11 languages. You can orientate your iPhone in landscape mode, divide your screen into two parts and view both sides of the conversation.

- Search through your iPhone for apps, contacts, files, messages, and web searches from a single destination which results in prompt matches.
- Multitask with Picture in Picture allowing you to keep using Netflix, watch videos or make FaceTime calls while you use another app.
- In the Messages app, pin a conversation, mention someone in a conversation and reply to specific people in a conversation while making use of inline replies to send messages in a group conversation.
- Create your own memoji characters with templates for different hairstyles and headwear styles.
- The revamped Maps to get directions for cycling routes and discovering new locations including restaurants, busy streets, and electric vehicle charging units.
- Improved Camera app that allows you to take quick videos, change the video settings (resolution and frame rate) and take mirrored selfies.
- The Photos app allows you to filter and sort your pictures in collections and albums. You can also caption the photos and videos for ease of locating them. The new photos app displays pictures and videos in the photo library by days, months, and years to make it easier to check through the gallery.
- Additional control with the new Privacy setting allowing you to only share your location within an app and a notification at the top of the iPhone screen display anytime an app is accessing your microphone or camera.

- CarPlay to get directions, make calls, listen to music and review your calendar from your vehicle's display with a lot of fancy wallpapers. CarPlay can be used with different app types.

- A digital Car Key available in the Wallet app such that you can go from one place to another without the actual car keys. Once the iPhone is close to the car door, it can unlock it and when placed on the reader or wireless charger, the iPhone can start the car.

- FaceTime can identify sign languages. Once a participant of a group call is making a sign language, the person is recognized. You can also make eye contact during video calls when looking at the screen instead of the Camera.

- Be in touch with your home and manage the lighting temperature anytime during the day using the Adaptive lighting capability of the Home app. Once there is movement in pre-configured activity zones, you will be notified. Also, people that you have tagged previously in Photos app can be identified by your doorbell.

- Reminders app that notifies you of time, date, and event locations. You can also make use of iCloud to share your reminders with other iCloud users.

- Siri can now provide information to you without navigating away from what you are working on. Siri can also fetch answers from the web and send audio files from the Messages app. Siri's new voice is more natural and with time learns your personal preferences to make better suggestions when you search in podcasts, maps, and Safari.

- The native browser Safari is much more secure, robust, and with webpage language translations. Your privacy and security are the top priority. Privacy reports and warnings on suspicious sites are provided to enhance secure browsing and data protection.

- **Health app to help you set and achieve sleep goals. You can set sleep schedules and track your adherence.**

- **Sidecar is the continuity feature that enables you to use iPhone in landscape orientation as a secondary display for your Mac or a writing/drawing pad and extend your workspace. This implies that you can use Apple Pencil to draw, make designs and sketches, edit pictures or bring 3D models to life on your iPhone and use the content in real-time on your Mac.**

- **Automatically turn on dark mode at a particular time of the day. The dark mode makes the user interface into a black or deep-grey shade that makes it easier to use the device in dark or low light environments. Go to Settings > General > Appearance > Auto.**

- **New Fonts that can be downloaded from the App store and used in documents.**

Chapter 5: How to Use the Internet and How to Activate the Connection

Connect the iPhone to the Internet

Connect the iPhone to the Internet using an available Wi-Fi or mobile network.

Connect iPhone to a Wi-Fi network

1. Select Settings> Wi-Fi, then turn on Wi-Fi.
2. Tap one of the following:
3. Network: Enter the password if required.
4. Other: Connects to a hidden network. Enter the hidden network name, security type, and password.
5. If the Wi-Fi icon appears at the top of the screen, the iPhone connects to a Wi-Fi network. (To confirm this, you can view the webpage by opening safari) iPhone reconnects when you return to the same location.

Join a Personal Hotspot

If an iPad (Wi-Fi + mobile) or another iPhone shares a personal hotspot, you can use a mobile Internet connection.

1. Select Settings> Wi-Fi, then select the name of the device that shares your hotspot.
2. If you're prompted for a password on your iPhone, enter the

password in Settings> Mobile> Personal Hotspot on the personal hotspot sharing device.

Connect iPhone to a Mobile Network

iPhone automatically connects to your carrier's mobile data network if a Wi-Fi network isn't available. If the iPhone isn't connected, check the following:

1. Make sure the SIM card is turned on and unlocked. See Setting Up a Mobile Service on iPhone.
2. Select Settings> Mobile.
3. Make sure mobile data is turned on. For dual SIM models, tap Mobile data, then confirm the selected line. (You can only select one line for mobile data.) When you need an Internet connection, the iPhone does the following in order, until the connection is established: You are trying to connect to the most recently used available Wi-Fi network.
4. Displays a list of Wi-Fi networks within range and connects to the selected network.

Connects to the Operator's Mobile Data Network

If you do not have a Wi-Fi connection to the Internet, applications and services may transfer data over the operator's mobile network, which may incur additional charges. Contact your service provider for information about mobile data plan prices. To manage mobile data usage, see View or change mobile settings on iPhone.

Chapter 6: How to Move Data from Android to Your iPhone

Switching from Android to iPhone 12 is one of the best upgrades you can make. Luckily, there are several ways to move files from android to iPhone. Am going to give you one options to choose from.

Move to iOS

Apple has its app called "Move to iOS" to help its users transfer files from android to iPhone via Wi-Fi. You can securely move movies, contacts, pictures, videos, messages, mail accounts, web bookmarks, and calendars.

First, you have to install the app on both devices then follow these steps:

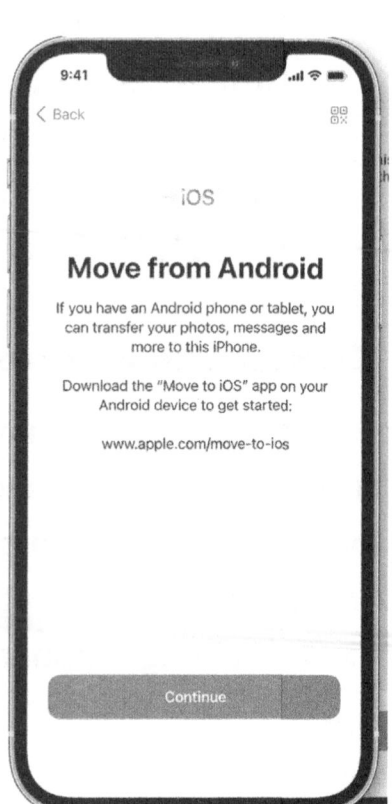

1. Set up your new iPhone until you get to the Apps & Data screen.
2. Tap on "Move Data from Android." On your android, download the 'Move to iOS app' and launch it.
3. Tap agree after going through the T&C, then tap "Next" in the find your code screen.
4. Tap Continue on your iPhone as well and wait until a code appears.
5. Enter the code that appears on your Android. Your Android will connect with your iPhone via Wi-Fi.

6. Mark the files you want to move and then tap Next.

Your android will now start moving the data to the iPhone and put the files in the right apps. Tap Continue iPhone Setup to finish the setup when the transfer is complete.

Chapter 7: Adding a Contact to Your Device

Open the Contacts app

1. Click on the + sign at the top right corner.
2. From the top section, you can enter all the necessary information like.
3. Contact's first name. Contact's last name. Contact's company.
4. Click on the green + symbol next to add a phone number.
5. Key in the contact's phone number.
6. Click on Done at the top right to save the contact.

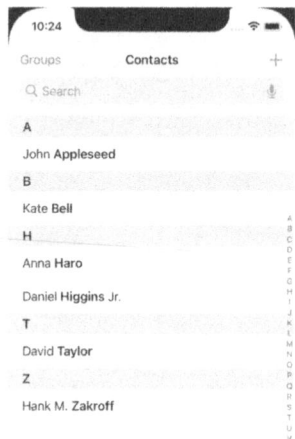

Updating an Existing Contact

1. Open the Contacts app
2. Click on the contact you want to update
3. Click on the Edit button at the top right corner

You can now add any other information such as phone numbers, email address, etc.

Finding an Existing Contact

1. Open the Contacts app
2. Click on the search bar
3. Enter the contact's name to find them

If it just so happens that you can't remember a contact's name but you are sure it's in your contact, you can find it by the first letter in their name.

1. Open the Contacts app.
2. Click on a letter on the right side of your screen.

Sharing a Contact

1. Go to the Contacts app
2. Click on the contact you want to share
3. Click on Share Contact

There are different ways to share the contact and you will have to use the one best suited for your intentions and follow the directions to send.

Assigning Photos to Contacts

1. Open the photos app
2. Click the photo you want to assign to a contact
3. Click the Share button at the bottom left of your screen
4. Click on Assign to Contact
5. Click on the contact you want to assign the photo to
6. Next, drag and pinch the photo to scale and set it as you like
7. Click choose at the bottom right of the screen
8. Click update at the top right of the screen

Deleting a Contact

1. Open the Contacts app
2. Click on the contact you want to delete
3. Click Edit at the top right corner
4. Navigate down to the bottom of the page
5. Click on Delete contact
6. Repeat step 6 again

Chapter 8: Managing Calls

How to Receive Calls

An incoming call can be answered, silenced, or declined. If a call is declined, it goes to voicemail. You can also use text to respond.

Tap on the call icon or drag the slider if the device is locked.

You can have your iPhone announce all incoming calls or only calls you receive while using headphones or Bluetooth in your car.

1. Open Settings
2. Go to Phone, and then to "Announce Calls."

Silence a Call

Press either the side button, Sleep/Wake button, or the volume button.

How to Decline a Call and Send It to Voicemail

You can either:

- Press the side or Sleep/Wake button twice quickly.
- Tap on the decline call button. Swipe up on the call banner.

How to Create a Default Reply

1. Open Settings, go to Phone, and then to "Respond with Text."
2. Tap any default message and replace it with your text.

How to Avoid Unwanted Calls

1. First, you need to download a spam blocking and call identifying app with good reviews, e.g., Nomorobo, TrueCaller, and

Hiya.

2. Once you have downloaded the app, go to Settings and then scroll down to "Call Blocking and Identification."

3. You should see the app you downloaded as an option in this section. Switch the toggle on so the app can start blocking your spam calls.

If the spam numbers are not on the app's list, it may not block all calls.

How to Setup Face Time

Apple's FaceTime app allows you to make video or audio calls to any of your friends and family, as long as they have an iPhone. Using your phone's front camera and FaceTime, you can talk to friends face to face. Or, you can switch to the rear camera so that you can both see what's in front of you. When setting up FaceTime, just make sure you have a cellular connection or a Wi-Fi connection. You can also choose which number you want your friends to use to contact you over FaceTime.

1. Head to Settings, then scroll down to FaceTime. Toggle on the FaceTime switch.

2. Sign in to FaceTime with your Apple ID or tap on Use another Apple ID and enter the details.

3. Select the phone number and/or email that you want your friends to contact you with via FaceTime.

4. Select a number or email for your Caller ID. Turn "FaceTime Live Photos" on to allow your friends to take live photos during FaceTime calls.

Note: You can block friends from contacting you over FaceTime, phone calls, messages, and email by tapping on "Blocked Contacts" and adding the contacts you want to block.

How to Make a Group Face Time Call

You can initiate a Group FaceTime call via the Face-Time app or the Messages app.

FaceTime App

1. Head to the FaceTime app and tap on the "+" plus button.
2. Type a name in the "To:" field and tap it. Continue typing the names of all the participants you want to chat with.
3. Tap the audio or video option when you are ready to place the call and participants will receive a notification that you want to FaceTime with them.

Block a Caller

To avoid FaceTime calls with particular individuals, you can block them on all your devices.

1. Go to FaceTime > Preferences > Blocked and clicking the Add Button + and selecting the names of the people to be blocked from your list of contacts.
2. When a contact is blocked, if they call you, you would not receive any notifications and the call will not be answered.

Chapter 9: Customize Messages

Apple has continued to push messages forward over the last few big OS releases, and iOS 14 is no different, with a huge pile of new features. The messages app has got an impressive overhaul to enhance your texting experience. There is a lot to discover from emoji search to revamped memoji and new options within group chats.

Pinned Conversations

Pinned conversations go right to the top of your messages, making them easy to keep track of. As usual, swipe to the left to Mute or Delete a conversation.

To use this feature:

1. Swipe from left to right on a conversation you want to pin
2. Tap the Pin icon

When you receive a message in a pinned conversation, it will appear at the top of the pin, and you can tap to open it. You can pin up to 9 conversations that sync across the messages app on your iPhone, iPad, and mac.

To unpin a chat:

1. Tap and hold the pinned conversation
2. Select the Unpin option.

Spice Up Your Messages with Special Effects

If you're trying to send a text, after you're done typing the message, if you 3D-touch on the send button (which is the press a bit hard on the message), it will bring up lots of effects that you can add to the message like slam, gentle, invisible ink, etc. These are added features to make messaging more fun and interesting. You can also experiment to see what works for you best.

Group Chats

You can now change the name and photo of a group conversation by tapping "Change Name and Photo" at the top of the group conversation. Before iOS 14, you could add a group name, but in this new interface, you can add a group name and a photo or an emoji.

At the top of the conversation, you'll see all the group members with the most recently active ones showing up as a larger icon.

To start a new conversation:

- Tap the "pen" icon at the top right of the messages screen
- Type in the name of the people you want to start a group chat with
- Type your message in the text field, and tap send

To add an icon to the group chat:

- Open the group conversation
- Tap on the Group icon at the top
- Tap the small "info" icon
- Tap "Change Name and Photo."

You can set a photo, memoji, or emoji as the group icon.

After you select a photo, tap Done.

Inline Replies

The messages app in iOS 14 allows you to reply directly to a specific message within a group chat as an inline reply. To do this:

1. Hold down on a particular message within the group chat
2. Tap reply
3. Type your reply and send

It will appear as a thread rather than another message within the entire conversation.

To view a particular message thread, just tap on it to expand.

Mentions

You can tag people within a group conversation.

1. Type a name in the message input field
2. Tap on the little bubble suggestion that will pop up
3. Type your message and send

The person mentioned receives a notification that he was mentioned even if he/she muted the conversation.

Emoji Search

This makes it easy to find the perfect expressions. To use this feature, tap the emoji icon on the keyboard, and you'll see a new search emoji field at the top of the keyboard.

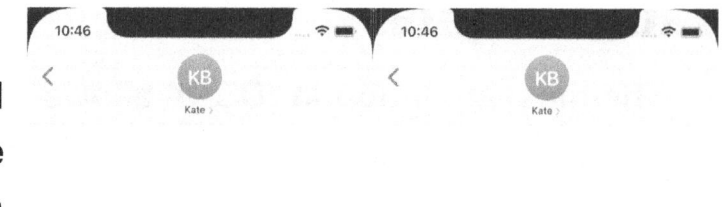

Keyboard Updates

The iOS 14 keyboard has device dictation. The keyboard will also display autofill suggestions from contacts, email addresses, phone numbers, and more.

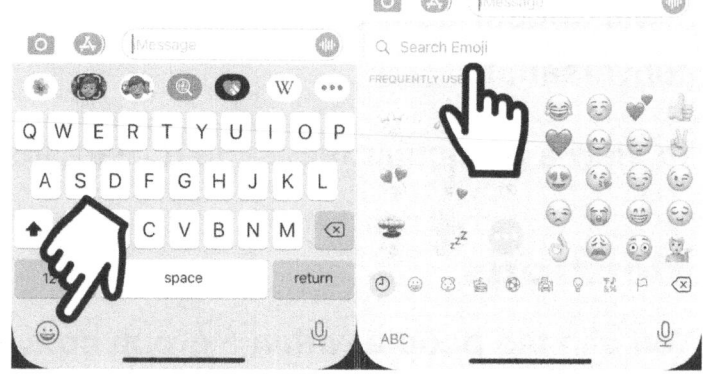

There are new dictionaries for French, German, Indonesian, English, Japanese, simplified Chinese, and polish English. There are also redesigned Japanese kana keyboards with easier input.

Chapter 10: Sync iPhone 12 with Computer

With iCloud, you can automatically update your photos, files, calendars, and more on any device that is signed in with your Apple ID. (You can even use a Windows PC to access your iCloud data on iCloud.com.) Other services like Apple Music allow you to access additional content on all of your devices. No need to sync with iCloud and services like Apple Music.

If you don't want to use iCloud or other services, you can connect iPhone to your Mac or Windows PC to sync the following items:

- **Albums**
- **Songs**
- **Playlists**
- **Movies**
- **TV shows**
- **Podcasts**
- **Books, and audiobooks**
- **Photos and videos**
- **Contacts and calendar**

Syncing is a great way to keep these items up to date between your computer and your iPhone.

NOTE: If you use iCloud or other services like Apple Music, the options to sync with your computer may not be available.

Set up Syncing Between Your Mac and iPhone

Steps:

1. Connect iPhone and your computer via USB.
2. Select your iPhone in the Finder sidebar on your Mac. Note: macOS 10.15 or higher is required to use the Finder to sync content. In earlier versions of macOS, use iTunes to sync with your Mac.
1. At the top of the window, click the type of content you want to sync (such as movies or books).
2. Select "Synchronize [content type] with [device name]."
3. By default, all items of a content type are in sync. However, you can also sync individual items, e.g. selected music, movies, books, or calendars. Repeat the above steps for each type of content you want to sync, then click Apply.
4. Your Mac will sync with your iPhone every time you connect.
5. To view or change sync options, select your iPhone in the Finder sidebar, then choose from the options at the top of the window.
6. Before you disconnect your iPhone from your Mac, press the Eject button in the Finder sidebar.

Set up Sync Between Your Windows Pc and Your iPhone

Steps:

1. Connect iPhone and your computer via USB.
2. In the iTunes application on your PC, click the iPhone button in the upper left corner of the iTunes window.
3. In the left sidebar, select the type of content you want to sync (for example, movies or books).
4. Select Synchronize to activate synchronization for this type of

item.

5. By default, all items of a content type are in sync. However, you can also sync individual items, e.g. selected music, movies, books, or calendars. Repeat the above steps for each type of content you want to put on your iPhone, then click Apply.

6. By default, your Windows PC syncs with your iPhone every time it connects; iTunes may ask you before syncing. If you don't want some items to sync, you can prevent them from syncing.

Turn On Wi-Fi Syncing

Steps:

1. Connect iPhone and your computer via USB.

2. Do one of the following:
   - In the Finder sidebar on your Mac: Select your iPhone, click General at the top of the window, and then select "Show this [device] if you have Wi-Fi."
   - NOTE: macOS 10.15 or later is required to use Finder to enable Wi-Fi syncing. In earlier versions of macOS, use iTunes to turn on Wi-Fi syncing.
   - In the iTunes application on a Windows PC: Click the iPhone button in the upper left of the iTunes window, click "Summary" and select "Sync with this [device] over Wi-Fi" (under "Options "). Click Apply. By default, the computer will sync your selected content to the iPhone when the iPhone is plugged in and connected to your Mac or iTunes on your Windows PC via Wi-Fi.

Chapter 11: Turn on iCloud backup

Have you already set up iCloud on your device? Usually, the service configuration is done when you link your new Apple device for the first time or update any device with the new device.

Regardless, if you have stopped doing this configuration process, we have done this step by step to help you solve that problem.

How to Sign in/out to iCloud on iPhone 12

1. Select the settings preference on your device's home screen.
2. Within "Settings," select the item "iCloud."
3. In the iCloud configuration screen, input your Apple ID and password (the same used in the AppStore and iTunes).
4. Then, press the "Start" button. If you do not have an Apple ID, press the "Get a Free Apple ID" button and fill in the data that will be requested.
5. When starting the service, you'll have to answer whether you want the iPhone location to be activated.
6. Confirm by pressing the "OK" button or cancel the "Do not allow" button. This action configures or not the proficiency to locate the device in case of loss or theft.
7. On the iCloud services screen, tap the Enable/Disable button for each service you want to make use of.
8. If you'd like to Activate Device Backup on iCloud, tap on "Storage and Backup" and then activate the item "iCloud Backup."

Now everything done on the device will be synchronized with iCloud automatically whenever a connection is available.

How to Use a Cloud Backup on iPhone 12

By default, iOS already backs up the iPhone to iCloud, and, optionally, it is also possible to back up to iTunes - in both cases, see how to check if everything is right. After backing up, you also have to know how to restore it.

Backing up your content via iCloud on the iPhone 12 isn't as tricky both for iCloud and iTunes. Upon seeing an error like "a newer version of iOS is required," try setting up the phone as a new one (without restoring a backup), updating the system, and then formatting the iPhone again.

Before seeing how to restore the backup, check Cloud for an active backup in the case that you've not yet reset the device.

Then, format the phone and discern the steps below:

1. Turn on the iPhone and go through the "Hello" screen. If you haven't reached it yet, format your phone.
2. Choose the option Restore from an iCloud Backup Do log in to iCloud and select a backup
3. Enter your Apple ID data to restore iTunes purchases.
4. Wait for the iCloud restoration to complete. Ready! Your iPhone should be as it was before.

How to Manage Apple ID and Cloud Settings

Your Apple ID account is what you'll use to access Apple services such as iTunes and App Store, Apple Books, etc. You can store and share your apps, photos, documents, videos, music, and more on iCloud and keep your files updated on all your devices.

How to Set Up iCloud

You'll be asked if you want to use iCloud Drive to store your data when you update your iOS operating system or start using a new iPhone. If you tap 'Yes,' then you are all set. If during setup, you have tapped "No" but you have decided to use iCloud Drive, you can still manually activate it.

1. Go to setting and tap on your Apple ID banner.
2. Tap iCloud. Switch on the iCloud Drive and log in with your iCloud account.

How to View Your iCloud Account Info

You can view your contact details, registered devices, security, and iCloud payment setup.

1. Go to setting and tap on your Apple ID banner.
2. Scroll down and select a device you want to view or remove from your account. Tap on "Remove from Account."
3. Scroll up and tap the details you want to change. You can change your name, phone number, email address, birthday, password, registered phone number.
4. Tap on "Payment & Shipping" to change your credit card number, expiration date, and shipping address.

How to manage iCloud Sync Permissions

You can connect to iCloud from third-party apps and access files from any device. You can manually revoke permission at any time even if you used a third-party app to set up iCloud.

1. Go to settings and tap on your Apple ID banner.
2. Tap iCloud. Here, you can turn the app you want to allow or revoke iCloud Drive syncing on or off.

How to Sign Out of iCloud

1. Go to settings and tap on your Apple ID banner.
2. Scroll to Sign Out and tap it. Tap on Sign Out again if prompted.
3. To store iCloud data on your device, tap Save on my iPhone or tap "Delete from my iPhone" to delete data.

iCloud Backup

Launch Settings > Tap on your Apple ID profile listing at the top > Go to iCloud > iCloud backup

Chapter 12: Adjust the iPhone Volume

Adjust the iPhone Volume

While on the phone making calls or listening to songs or other media, the buttons on the side of the iPhone adjust the volume. Otherwise, the keys control the volume of the ringtone, alarms, and other sound effects. You can also use Siri to increase or decrease the volume.

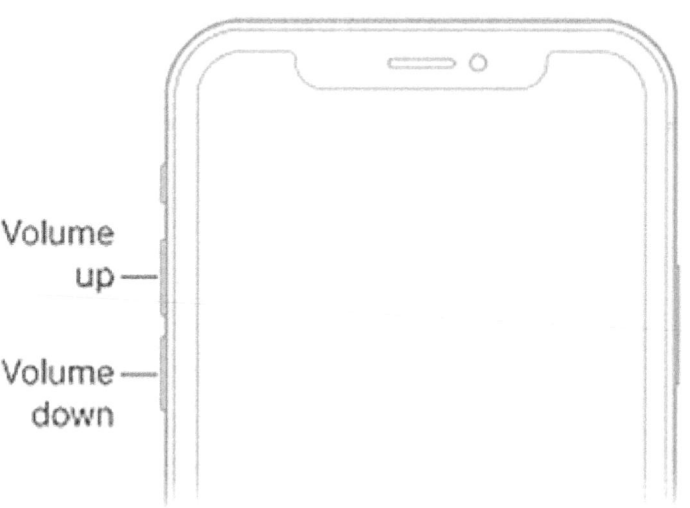

Ask Siri. Switch up the volume or Turn down the volume. Learn how to ask Siri.

For important information on preventing hearing damage, see Important iPhone Safety Information.

Lock the Ring Volume and Alarm Volume in Settings

1. Go to Settings.
2. Tap Sounds and Haptics (supported models) or Sounds (other iPhone models).
3. Turn off Change with.
4. Adjust the volume in the control center.

If the iPhone is locked or you are using an app, you can adjust the volume in Control Center.

1. Open the Control Center, then drag the volume slider.
2. Limits the headphone volume

You can choose to limit the maximum headphone volume for music and videos.

1. Go to Settings.
2. Tap Sounds and Haptics (supported models) or Sounds (other iPhone models).
3. Press Mute, turn on Mute, and then drag the slider to select the maximum decibel level for the headphone sound.

The Mute Loud screen, which is a button to turn the sound on or off, displays a slider to change the maximum decibel level and the selected limit of 85 decibels.

If you have turned on the screen time in Settings, you can prevent the volume of the headphones from changing. Select Settings> Screen time> Content and privacy restrictions> Mute and select Disable.

Temporarily Mute Calls, Alerts, and Alerts

Open the control center and press Do not disturb. See Do Not Disturb iPhone.

Set iPhone to Call or Silent Mode

1. To set iPhone to ring mode, turn off the ring/mute switch.
2. Top of the front of the iPhone with the display pointing to the Ring/Silent switch.

In-ring mode, the iPhone plays all sounds. In silent mode the orange switch, the iPhone does not ring or play alarms or other sound effects (but the iPhone can still vibrate).

Alerts, audio apps like Music, and many games play sounds through the built-in speaker, even when the iPhone is in silent mode. In some regions, the sound effects of the camera, voice memos, and emergency alerts can be played back even if the Ring/Mute switch is muted.

Swap the Sounds and Vibrations of the iPhone

In Settings, you can change iPhone sounds when you receive a call, SMS, voicemail, email, reminder, or other types of notification.

On supported models, you will feel a touch—called haptic feedback—after performing certain actions, such as when you press and hold the camera icon on the Home screen.

Adjust the sound and Vibration Options

1. Move to Settings> Sounds & Happiness (for supported models) or Sounds (for other iPhone models).
2. To adjust the volume for all sounds, drag the slider under Ringtones and Alerts.
3. To set sounds and vibration patterns for sounds, tap a sound type, such as a ringtone or text sound.
4. Do one of the following:
   - Select a sound (scroll to see all). Ringtones are used to play incoming calls, time alarms, and a timer; text tones are used for text messages, new voicemail, and other notifications.
   - Tap Vibrate, then select a vibration pattern or tap Create new vibration to create your own.

Turn Haptic Feedback on or off

1. Go to Settings> Sounds & Haptics.
2. Turn System Haptics on or off.

3. **When System Haptics is turned off, you will not hear or feel vibrations from incoming calls and alerts.**

Tip: If you do not hear or see incoming calls and alerts while waiting for them, open the Control Center and make sure Do Not Disturb is turned on. If the Do Not Disturb button is highlighted, press it to turn off Do Not Disturb. (If the Do Not Disturb feature is turned on, the Do Not Disturb icon also appears in the status bar.)

Chapter 13: How to Download Apps Like WhatsApp

How to Download and Install Apps

Apps installed from the App Store either appear on your Home screen or on a subsequent screen of apps.

First, you need to search for cool apps to get them:

1. Head to the App Store and tap on the magnifying glass at the bottom of your screen (the search button).
2. Type in the app you want to search for and tap the search button.

How to Download Apps and Games

1. Tap on the app or game you searched for (it could be free or you'll need to purchase it).
2. If it is free tap on Get it or tap on the price if it is paid.
3. Next, activate Touch ID by Double-clicking the side button for Face ID or place your finger on the Home button.

How to Install WhatsApp

WhatsApp is an instant messaging application that has been part of Facebook since 2016. In my view, the most widely used messaging app in the world is WhatsApp. Hence, installing them on your Apple iPhone 12 is very useful.

This chapter will teach you how to install and configure WhatsApp on an iPhone 12 models in minutes with simple steps:

1. **To Install WhatsApp on your iPhone 12 is very simple and can be accomplished just in few minutes. To begin, search for the App Store app on the Apple iPhone 12 home screen and tap on it to open.**

2. **Click the magnifying glass or search button at the bottom right of the iPhone 12 screen.**

3. **Enter WhatsApp Messenger in the text field under Search and select the first option or press Search on the keyboard. Search the App Store**

4. **Click Get to begin downloading and installing the WhatsApp messaging application on your iPhone 12. Depending on your internet connection, it will take a few minutes or seconds as you will have to download several megabytes.**

5. **When the installation is complete, the Open option will appear. When you want to return to the home screen of your Apple iPhone 12, you will see the green WhatsApp icon on this screen. If you can't find it, drag to find it to the right.**

6. **Open WhatsApp: Accept the WhatsApp Terms of Service, click Accept, and Continue. Accept**

7. **Enter your phone number and make sure the prefix matches your country. You will receive an SMS with this phone number, so it must be correct and you must have access to this number. If it is the phone number of your iPhone 12, the app reads the SMS automatically and confirms if it is correct. You do not have to enter the code received via SMS.**

8. **Click OK or Next.**

9. **Configure WhatsApp: Enter your username, the name you would like to show your contacts on WhatsApp. Very easy to upload a picture and be recognized by anyone.**

10. **If you click Next, WhatsApp is already installed and configured**

on your iPhone 12 with the iOS 14 operating system. Write in your contacts by pressing the + key.

In your iPhone 12 you can store WhatsApp photos and videos thanks to the internal memory of 128 GB 6 GB RAM, 256 GB 6 GB RAM, 512 GB 6 GB RAM.

You can connect your iPhone 12 via Wi-Fi thanks to its connectivity Wi-Fi 802.11 a/b/g/n/ac 6, dual-band, hotspot, and download all photos and videos from WhatsApp.

If you need to check WhatsApp from your iPhone 12 anywhere, you can use HSPA 42.2 / 5.76Mbps, LTE-A 5G, EV-DO Rev. A 3.1Mbps network connection.

You can also make video calls from your Apple iPhone 12 via WhatsApp, thanks to the 12 MP SL 3D, f / 2.2, 23 mm (wide), selfie (depth / biometric sensor) or front camera and the super capacitive touchscreen Retina XDR OLED, 1B colors 6.7 inches, 110.3 cm2, 1242 x 2688 pixels, a screen with a ratio of 19.5: 9 (density ~ 442 PPI).

How to Manually Update Games and Apps

Go to the App Store and tap on your Profile icon. Head to "Update" for apps that need updates.

How to Run Automatic Update

1. Launch Settings and tap on iTunes and App Store.
2. Scroll to automatic downloads and switch App Updates on.

How to Disable App Updates Over Cellular

If you are concerned about using your data to download updates, especially if automatic updates are on, you should disable them.

1. Head to Settings and tap on iTunes and App Store.
2. Under Cellular Data, turn the Automatic Downloads switch off.

How to Subscribe to Apple Arcade

1. Head to the app store and look down to the bottom you will see the arcade button.
2. You can do a free trial for a month. Click try free and agree to the "T&C"
3. Tap on Subscribe to start a monthly subscription. Review the subscription detail and confirm with your ID.

How to Cancel your Apple Arcade Subscription

1. Go to App Store and tap on your profile icon.
2. Tap on Subscriptions, then on "Apple Arcade" and then tap on Cancel Subscription.

You can't play any Arcade games after you have canceled your subscription. You can re-subscribe to play the games and regain access to your gameplay data. You might lose some of your gameplay data if you don't re-subscribe on time.

How to Close Apps

1. Head to the app and hold the long line at the end of your screen with a finger.
2. Slide the line upwards to close the app.

How to Close Multiple Apps

1. Open your home screen and slide the screen upwards from the

bottom with your fingers.

2. You will see all the apps you opened running in the background.

3. Slide each app upwards to close them.

Switch Between Apps

You can use multiple apps at the same time and transit from one to the other, picking up where you left off each time.

Swipe from the bottom of the screen upwards and stop at the Center of the screen while using an iPhone with Face ID while you simply double press the Home button on iPhones with Touch ID to view all your open apps. Then click on the app you want to use.

Search Through Your iPhone

You can conduct searches on your iPhone for apps, contacts, files, and even information on the internet. The apps to be included in Search can be added manually. Go to Settings > Siri & Search > Click on app > Turn on 'Show in Search.'

To run the actual search, swipe down from the Center of the Home screen, to reveal the Search field and type in the search term. You can then Hide the keyboard and see more results on the screen, open a suggested app, get more information about a search suggestion or start a new search.

Chapter 14: Family Sharing

Set up Family Sharing on iPhone

Family Sharing requires you (the host) to sign in with your Apple ID and affirm the Apple ID you utilize for the iTunes Store, App Store, and Apple Books (you generally use the same Apple ID for everything).

1. Go to Settings> [your name]> Family Sharing and follow the onscreen instructions to set up your family group. You can include family members or better still, create an account for a child.

2. Touch a feature you want to share and follow the onscreen instructions.

For more information on Family Sharing features, see the following:

- **Purchases: You can share purchases from iTunes Store, App Store, Apple Books, and Apple TV.**
- **Locations: When you share your location with family members, they can use the Find My app to view your location and help locate a lost device.**
- **Kids Features: You can manage your children's spending and control how they use their Apple devices.**

Depending on the features you choose, you may be required to set up a subscription. If you choose to share App Store purchases, music, movies, TV, and books with your family members, you agree to pay for any purchases they make while in the family group. Adult and teen family members can turn off shopping sharing themselves.

You can also share photos, calendars, and more with family members.

Add a Family Member

The family group organizer can add a family member.

1. Proceed to Settings. Then input [your name]> Family Sharing and click Add Member.
2. Tap Invite people and follow the onscreen instructions.

You can send the invitation via AirDrop, Messages, or Email. If you are close to the family member, you can also tap Personal Invite and ask the family member to enter their Apple ID and password on the screen labeled "Family Apple ID Family Member."

Create an Apple ID for a Child

The organizer, parent, or guardian can create an Apple ID for a child in a family group.

1. Proceed to Settings. Then input [your name]> Family Sharing and click Add Member.
2. Do one of the following:
   - If you are the organizer: tap Add member, tap Create an account for a child and follow the onscreen instructions.
   - If you are a parent or guardian: tap Add a child and follow the onscreen instructions.

See What You Share with Your Family

You can see what you're sharing with your family and adjust the sharing settings at any time. Features that you share with your family appear on top of the features that you have not shared.

1. Proceed to Settings. Then input [your name]> Family Sharing.
2. Tap a function and do one of the following:
   - If you have not configured the feature: Follow the on-screen instructions to configure it.
   - If you have configured the feature: Check and adjust the sharing settings.

Log Out or Turn off Family Sharing

1. Proceed to Settings. Then input [your name]> Family sharing> [your name].
2. Do one of the following:
   - Disband family group: Tap Stop using family. Only the organizer can dissolve the family group.
   - Stop family sharing: Tap Stop family sharing.

Young children cannot be separated from a family group and must move to another family before you dissolve yours.

Download Purchases from Family Members on iPhone

If you arrange or set up Family Sharing, up to five members of your family and yourself can share buys from the App Store, Apple Books, iTunes Store, and Apple TV.

Adult and teen family members can turn off shopping sharing themselves. The family organizer may also require children in the family group to request approval for free purchases or downloads.

After purchase, an item is added to the original family member's account and eligible purchases are shared with the rest of the family.

1. Download Shared Purchases from the iTunes Store
2. Open the iTunes Store, tap More, then tap Purchased.
3. Choose a family member.
4. Click a category for an instant, Music>tap a purchased item, and then tap the Redownload button to download it.

Download Shared Purchases from the App Store

1. Open the App Store.
2. Touch the My Account button or your profile picture in the top right.
3. Tap Purchased, choose a family member, and then touch the Redownload button next to a purchased item to download it.
4. Download Shared Purchases from Apple Books
5. Open the Books app.
6. At the top right, tap the Account button or your profile picture.
7. Tap a family member's name in Family Shopping, and then tap a category (for example, Books or Audiobooks).
8. Tap All, Recent Purchases, or a Genre, and then tap the Redownload button next to a purchased item to download it.

Download (Boot-Up) Shared Purchases from the Apple TV App

1. Open the Apple TV app.
2. Tap Library, tap Family Sharing, and choose a family member.
3. Click a category for an instant, TV shows or movies or a genre>tap a purchased item, and then click the Download button to download it.

Stop Sharing Purchases with Family Members on iPhone

With Family Sharing, the organizer can activate shopping sharing. Purchases made by family members from the iTunes Store, App Store, Apple Books, and Apple TV are charged directly to the organizer's Apple ID account.

If an adult and adolescent family members don't want to share purchase and billing information with family members, they can turn off the option to buy stock.

Note: The family organizer may also require children in the family group to request approval for free purchases or downloads.

1. Go to Settings> [your name]> Family Sharing.
2. Touch Share purchases and turn off Share purchases with family.

If the organizer wants to turn off shopping sharing entirely, they can tap Stop shopping sharing.

Activate Request Purchase for Children on iPhone

When you set up Family Sharing, the family organizer may require the children in the family group to request approval for free purchases or downloads. Purchases can be approved by the organizer or a parent or guardian in the household.

1. Go to Settings> [your name]> Family Sharing.
2. Tap Request purchase, and then do one of the following:
   - If there are no children in your household: touch Add Child or Create Child Account, then follow the onscreen instructions.

- If there is a child in your household: tap the child's name and activate Request to purchase.

Note: **Age limitations for Ask to Buy vary by region. In the United States, the family coordinator can activate Request Purchase for any relative younger than 18; for youngsters under 13 is activated as a matter of course (default).**

Set up Apple Cash Family on iPhone

With Family Sharing, the coordinator can make an Apple Cash represent a youngster in the family gathering and utilize the Wallet application to see the card balance, track exchanges, and breaking point to whom the kid can send cash.

1. Proceed to Settings. Then input [your name]> Family Sharing.
2. Tap Apple Cash and do one of the following:
   - If there is no child in your household: touch Add Child or Create Child Account and follow the onscreen instructions.
   - If there is a child in your household: tap the child's name, tap Set up Apple Cash, and follow the onscreen instructions.

Share Your Location with Family Members

Family Sharing allows you to share your location with members of your family group. When the family organizer sets up location sharing in Family Sharing settings, the organizer's location is automatically shared with all family members. Then it's up to family members to decide whether or not to share their location or whereabout.

If you share your location, your family members can see your location in

Find My, and if you lose your device, they can help you find it. You can also be notified when family members change locations, for example, if a child leaves school during school hours.

Note: To share your location, location services must be enabled in Settings> Privacy.

1. Go to Settings> [your name]> Family Sharing> Share location and enable Share my location.
2. If your iPhone is not currently sharing your location, tap Use this iPhone as my location.
3. Touch the name of a family member you want to share their location with, and then touch Share my location.
4. You can redo this step for each family member you intend to share your location or whereabouts with. Each family member will receive a message that they share their location and can choose to share their location with you.
5. To stop sharing your location with a family member, touch the family member's name, then touch Stop sharing my location.

You can also send or share your location while using the Messages application. Touch your family member's profile photo or name at the top of the conversation, touch the info button, and then touch Send my current location or Share my location.

Share a Personal Hotspot

With Family Sharing, you can share an Internet connection through a personal access point with members of your family group. If a member of your family group sets up a Personal Hotspot, other family members can use it without entering the password.

Find a Lost Relative's Device on iPhone

If you are part of a Family Sharing group and family members share their location with you, you can use the Find My app on your iPhone, iPad, iPod touch, or Mac or Find My iPhone on iCloud.com to find another member of the family. family. help find a lost device.

Set your iPhone to Be Found by a Family Member

A family member can help you find your lost iPhone by doing the following on the device before losing it:

- Enable location services: Go to Settings> Privacy and enable location services.
- Enable Find My iPhone: Go to Settings> [your name]> Find My> Find My iPhone and enable Find My iPhone, Find My Network, and Send Last Location.
- Share your location with family members: go to Settings> [your name]> Family sharing> Share location and enable Share my location.

Set Screen Time Via Family Sharing on iPhone

You can set screen time for a child in your family group through Family Sharing. This includes downtime, app usage assignments, contacts your child communicates with, content ratings, and more. Screen Time also allows you and your child to see how they use their devices and use that information to structure their device usage. To use Screen Time, your child must use a suitable device.

1. Proceed to Set. Then input [your name]> Family Sharing> Screen Time.
2. Click the name of a child in your family group>click Enable

Screen Time and adhere to the instructions on the screen.

Important: In the event, you set Screen Time for a child in Family Sharing and you can't remember the Family Screen Time passcode or password, you can reset it.

Family Management

1. Click the Family Member icon (+) and follow the on-screen instructions.
2. See if your family member agrees to the application. After you submit the invitation, you can check the status of the person under their name.
3. With your iPad, iPhone, Go to Settings> [Your Name]> Family Share.
4. The person's name has been chosen to see what the reception looks like. If you want to resubmit the invitation, choose to resubmit the call.

iMac

1. Select the Apple System> System Preferences list and click Family Share. If you are using the OS Cause or are already using it, select Apple> System Preferences> iCloud and click on Family Management.
2. The person's name will be chosen to see what the reception looks like. If you want to resubmit the invitation, choose to resubmit the call.

Join the family group

Accept or reject the application to access a family directly from your device. An application will be sent to you via email or comment. You can then respond directly by invitation. If you lose your email and text message, there is no problem. You can answer from your device settings or system preferences.

1. With your iPad, iPhone, Go to Settings> [Your Name]> Applicants.
2. To accept an invitation, follow the on-screen instructions.

Chapter 15: Safari

Generated version iOS 14 has a translation option in Safari, which translates the page into English, Spanish, Chinese, French, German, Russian, or Brazilian Portuguese, and has been added to update Apple's new translation program.

To access a website page in the Supported languages and translations section is as easy as clicking the "AA" button in the menu bar. Click Translate and the website page will automatically change the language on your phone.

Additional languages that you can translate can be added to the iPhone settings program.

Safari on OS 14 can track stored passwords by detecting data related to data breaches.

To illustrate this, Safari uses Safari duplication technology to verify your passwords, as opposed to a list of passwords that are considered secure and secure. If something crashes, you should notify Safari by giving us an idea to update your Apple login or generate a secure password automatically.

Websites that make money or use marketing networks for these purposes are just like any other website that uses analytics services like Google Analytics to collect information about website user behavior and project improvements.

In Safari on the iPhone, if you see a video clip, you can browse another website to view it in window mode or click a button to do something on your iPhone While the videotape is playing.

How to Get Started with Websites

If you're typing a URL like Apple.com when you're downloading the search interface on an iPhone, you can click the "Go" button to open the website directly without typing. When linking to search results.

Easy Integration

Apple developers have created new tools for transferring website accounts to Apple, making it more convenient for iPhone, and iPad users who want to change the login with Apple.

Search Permission

To provide personalized content, you need to obtain user consent for websites and applications you wish to search through websites. Enable the app to search or request not to have both options for the app, but the app is attached in a confidential statement so you can stay up to date on the app usage and website browsing habits.

Safari Translate

With iOS 14, you can translate websites to your iPhone's language. The supported languages are English, Spanish, German, French, Portuguese, Russian, and Chinese.

1. Tap the "aA" icon.
2. Tap "translate to English."
3. To go back to the original language, tap the translate icon.
4. Then tap View Original.

Picture in Picture

You can watch videos in the Picture in Picture mode using safari.

1. Enable full screen and Swipe Down
2. Privacy Report.
3. Tap on the "aA" icon.
4. Tap Privacy Report.
5. Tap Prevent Cross-Site Tracking.

Safari goes a step further with its intelligent tracking prevention. It will show you exactly which trackers it prevented on what sites with a detailed privacy report.

1. Tap on the "aA" icon.
2. Tap Privacy Report.

It displays a list of all trackers that were stopped on each website. Tap on each website to see the trackers.

Password Security Monitoring and Recommendations

1. Go to Settings.
2. Go to Passwords.
3. Tap on Security Recommendations.

Safari will alert you to change passwords that appeared in a data breach, are weak, or are reused.

If you're using Apple's KeyChain, go to your Settings, and then go down to Passwords. This will give you security recommendations of passwords that may or may not be compromised and gives you the option to change them.

Safari Tips and Tricks

- Tap and hold the Tabs icon to bring up more options.
- Tap and hold the Bookmark icon to bring up more options.
- Tap and hold the "back" icon to bring up more options.
- Tap and hold the "forward" icon to bring up more options.
- Tap the Tabs icon.
- Tap and hold Done to close all open tabs.
- Tap and hold + to see the recently closed websites.

Chapter 16: Use Camera Correctly

iPhone 12 has sets of 12mp cameras. iPhone 12 and 12 mini each have a 12mp front camera, 12mp wide-angle, and standard cameras. A 12mp 2x zoom and a LiDAR scanner are added to the 12 Pro, while the Pro Max has 2.5x zoom and LiDAR. LiDAR bounces light pulses off objects to determine distance. It makes augmented reality apps more fluid; when taking pictures, it speeds up and improves autofocus in dim light and enables the 12 Pro's striking low light portrait mode.

Apple's Night mode takes out most of its competition. The 12 Pro's 2x zoom gives clarity that is impossible with iPhone 12 and 11 digital zoom and is even a little better than the Galaxy Note 20. The real difference is in Night Mode. iPhone 12 series supports the night mode on its front cameras. iPhone 12 in short, provides very good cameras. If you are unhappy with the low light performance of your older device, you will experience a better upgrade with this new device. iPhone 12 also supports Dolby Vision HDR video recording.

Take a Picture

Learn how to take great pictures with your iPhone camera. Choose from camera modes such as Photo, Video, Pano, Timed, Slo-mo, and Portrait (supported models). Enhance your photos with camera features like night mode, live photos, filters, and bursts.

Ask Siri. Say something like "Open the camera." Learn how to ask Siri.

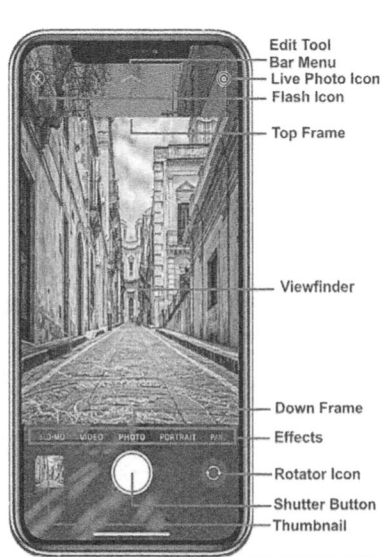

Edit Tool
Bar Menu
Live Photo Icon
Flash Icon
Top Frame

Viewfinder

Down Frame
Effects
Rotator Icon
Shutter Button
Thumbnail

Camera in photo mode, with other modes, left and right below the viewfinder. The Flash, Night Mode, Camera Controls, and Live Photo buttons appear at the top of the screen. The photo and video view buttons are located in the lower-left corner. The Capture button is in the bottom center, and the Camera Chooser Back button is in the lower right corner.

Photo is the normal mode you see when you open the camera. You can take still pictures in Photo mode. Swipe left or right to select another model, such as Video, Pan, Timed, Beat, and Portrait.

Touch the home screen or swipe left from the lock screen to open the camera in photo mode.

Press the shutter button or press a volume button to take the picture.

Note: For your safety, a green dot appears at the top right of the screen when using the camera. See Checking Access to Hardware Features.

Turn the Flash On or Off

On iPhone 12, press the Flash button to turn the flash on or off. Or tap Camera Controls, then tap Flash below the frame to select Auto, on, or off.

Set a timer

Tap Timer

Zoom in or out

To zoom in or out, open the Camera app, and tap the screen.

For iPhone models with dual and triple-camera systems, switch between 1x, 2x, 2.5x and .5x to quickly zoom in or out (depending on model). To zoom more precisely, press and hold the zoom controls, and drag the slider to the right or left.

Selfie

Take a selfie with the front camera in photo or portrait mode.

1. Switch to the front camera by touching the camera selector Rear-face button or the camera selector Rear-facing button (depending on model).
2. Hold the iPhone in front of you. Tip: On iPhone 12 and iPhone 11, you can increase the field of view by tapping the arrows within the frame.
3. Press the shutter button or press a volume button to take the picture.

To create a mirrored selfie that captures the image as you see it inside the camera, go to Settings> Camera and turn on the Mirror Front Camera feature.

Adjust the Camera's Focus and Exposure

Before taking a picture, the iPhone automatically adjusts focus and exposure, and Face Detection balances exposure between many faces. Follow these steps to manually adjust focus and exposure:

1. Touch the screen to display the autofocus area and exposure setting.
2. Touch the location where you want to move the focus area.
3. Drag the exposure adjustment knob up or down next to the focus area to adjust the exposure.

To lock manual focus and exposure settings for the following images, touch and hold the focus area until AE/AF lock is displayed; tap the screen to unlock the settings.

Take Pictures in Low Light with Night Mode

For iPhone 12 the night mode captures details and illuminates your photos in low light. In night mode, the exposure length is determined automatically, but you can experiment with manual control.

For iPhone 12 models, night mode is available on the front camera for selfies, Ultra Wide (0.5x), and Wide (1x) cameras.

1. Select Photo Mode. In low light, night mode automatically turns on: the night mode button at the top of the screen turns yellow, and a number appears next to the night mode button to indicate how many seconds the camera takes to take pictures.
2. To experiment with night mode, press the night mode button, then use the slider below the frame to select between Auto and Max timers. In the case of Auto, the time is determined automatically; Max spends the longest time. The selected setting is retained by recording the next night mode.
3. Press the shutter button and hold the camera still to take the picture.
4. The crosshairs appear in the frame when the iPhone detects movement during shooting - adjust the crosshair to reduce movement and improve shooting.
5. To stop recording in night mode, press Stop under the slider.

Take a Live Photo

Live Photo captures what happens just before and after the photo is taken, including sound.

1. Select Photo Mode.
2. Press the Live Photo button to turn Live Photos on or off.
3. Press the shutter button to take the picture.

4. You can choose to add effects to Live Photos, such as Loop and Bounce. See Edit live photos on the iPhone.

Take a Picture with a Filter

Select Photo or portrait mode, and then do one of the following:

1. Tap Camera Controls and then Filters. For models earlier, tap Filters at the top of the screenDuring the display, slide the filters to the right or left to preview; press one to select.
2. You can remove or change the image filter in Images. See Restoring an Edited Image.

Take Continuous Pictures

Burst mode takes multiple high-speed shots, so you can choose from a variety of shots. You can take continuous pictures with the rear and front camera.

1. To take quick pictures, slide the shutter button to the left on iPhone 12 or press and hold for models earlier. The counter shows how many shots you have taken.
2. Lift your finger to stop.
3. To select the images you want to keep, tap the Burst thumbnail, then tap Select.
4. Below the thumbnails, gray dots indicate suggested images for preservation.
5. Tap the circle at the bottom right of each photo you want to save as a photo, then tap Done.
6. To delete the entire series, tap the thumbnail, then tap Delete.

Tip: To take a series of pictures, press and hold the volume up key. Go to Settings> Camera and turn on Serial Volume Up

Adjust the Camera Focus and Exposure

Before a photograph is taken, the iPhone camera automatically sets the concentration and exposure, and face identification adjusts the exposure of numerous faces. Do the following in the event you intend to manually adjust the focus and exposure:

1. Tap the screen to display the autofocus area and exposure settings.
2. Tap where you want to move the focus area.
3. Next to the focus area, pull the Adjust exposure button either up or down to adjust the exposure.
4. Touch the Camera Control button, touch the Exposure button, and then move the slider to adjust the exposure. The exposure will be locked until the next time you open the camera. To keep the exposure control so that it does not reset when you open the Camera, go to Settings> Camera> Keep settings and turn on Exposure adjustment.

Snap Photos in Low Light with Night Form

On the iPhone 12 models, Night mode captures more detail and makes your images brighter in low light. The duration of the exposure in Night mode is determined automatically, but you can experiment with the manual controls.

On iPhone 12 models, night mode is available on the front selfie camera, ultra-wide-angle (0.5x), and wide-angle (1x) camera. On iPhone 11 models, night mode is only available on the panoramic camera (1x).

Select the photo mode. In low light situations, night mode is activated automatically: the night mode button at the top of the screen turns yellow and a number appears next to the night mode button to indicate how many seconds the camera takes to shoot.

To experiment with night mode:

1. Tap the Night mode button and use the slider below the frame to choose between automatic and maximum timers. Auto determines the time automatically; Max uses the longest time. The settings you choose will be retained for your next Night mode shot.
2. Tap the shutter button and hold the camera steady to take your photo.
3. The visors will appear in the frame if your iPhone detects motion while capturing; raise the visor to reduce movement and improve the shot.
4. To stop taking a photo in night mode halfway through capture, tap the stop button below the slider.

Take a Panoramic Photo

Use Pano mode to take landscapes or other photos that don't fit on your camera screen.

1. Choose panoramic mode and tap the shutter button.
2. Slowly turn in the direction of the arrow and hold it on the centerline.
3. To end, just tap the shutter button again.
4. To access the opposite direction, touch the arrow. Rotate iPhone to landscape view to pan vertically. You can also reverse the direction of a vertical tray.

Record Videos with Your iPhone Camera

Use the camera to record videos on your iPhone and switch modes to record slow-motion and time-lapse videos.

Note: For your privacy, a green dot will appear in the upper right corner of the screen when the camera is in use.

Record a Video

1. Select video mode.
2. Tap the record button or press one of the volume buttons to start recording. While recording, feel free to do the below:
   - Press the white shutter button to take a photo.
   - Nip the screen to zoom in and out.
   - For a more precise zoom on models with dual and triple-camera systems, hold down 1x and drag the slider to the left.
3. Touch the record button or press one of the volume buttons to stop recording.

By default, it records videos at 30 fps (frames per second). Depending on your model, you can choose different video resolution and frame rate settings in Settings> Camera> Record Video.

On iPhone 12 models, iPhone records HDR videos and shares HDR videos with devices running iOS 13.4, iPadOS 13.4, macOS 10.15.4 or higher; other devices are receiving an SDR version of the same video. To disable HDR recording, go to Settings> Camera> Record Video and turn off HDR video.

Record a Slow Motion Video

When you record a video in slow motion mode, your video will be recorded normally and you will see the slow-motion effect when you play it back. You can also edit your video so the slow-motion action starts and stops at a time of your choosing.

1. Choose a slow-motion mode.
2. On iPhone 12 models, you can tap the Camera Selector button on the back to record with the front camera in slow motion mode.
3. Tap the record button or press one of the volume buttons to start recording.
4. You can touch the shutter button to take a photo while recording.
5. Tap the record button or press one of the volume buttons to stop recording.

Depending on your model, you can change the frame rate and slow-motion resolution. To alter your slow-motion recording settings, proceed to Settings. Then go to Camera and tap Record slow motion.

Tip: Use quick switches to adjust video resolution and frame rate while recording.

Capture a Time-Lapse Video

Capture images at selected intervals to create a time-lapse video of an experience over some time, such as a sunset or flowing traffic.

1. Select the time-lapse mode.
2. Place your iPhone where you want to capture a moving scene.
3. Touch the record button to start recording; tap it again to stop recording.

Tip: On iPhone 12 models, use a tripod to capture time-lapse video with more detail and clarity when recording in low-light situations.

Take Portrait Photos with Your iPhone's Camera

With the camera on models that help portrait mode, you can apply a profundity of field impact that keeps your subject—individuals, pets, items, and more—in concentration while making a perfectly obscured foundation.

Take a Photo in Portrait Mode

1. Choose a portrait mode.
2. Follow the tips on the screen to frame your subject in the yellow portrait frame.
3. Drag the vertical light slider to choose a light effect:
   - **Natural light:** The face is in focus against a blurred background.
   - **Studio light:** The face is very bright and the picture looks generally clean.
   - **Contour Light:** The face has dramatic shadows with highlights and low lights.
   - **Stage light:** The face is lit with a spotlight on deep black background.
   - **Stage Light Mono:** The impact is like Stage Light, yet the photograph is in exemplary highly contrasting.
4. Tap the screen catch or button to snap the picture.

After taking a photo in portrait mode, you can remove the portrait mode effect if you don't like it. Open the photo in the Photos app, tap Edit, then tap Portrait to turn the effect on or off.

Use Camera Settings On iPhone

Learn how to use the camera settings on your iPhone.

Align Your Shots

To display a grid on the camera screen that you can use to straighten your footage, go to Settings> Camera and enable Grid.

After snapping a photo, you can utilize the editing tools in the Photos app to align pix and adjust the horizontal and vertical perspective.

Save Camera Settings

You can keep the settings for the last used camera mode, filter, exposure, depth, and Live Photo so they won't be reset the next time you open the Camera.

5. Go to Settings> Camera> Keep Settings.
6. Enable one of the following options:
   - Camera Mode: Keep the last camera mode you used, such as Video or Pano.
   - Creative Controls: Keep the last settings you used for the filter, lighting option
   - Exposure adjustment: Keep the exposure adjustment setting
   - Live Photo: Keep Live Photo settings.

Adjust the Volume of the Shutter Sound

Adjust the volume of the shutter sound with the volume buttons on the side of your iPhone. Or, when the Camera is open, swipe down from the upper right corner of the screen to open Control Center, and then drag the volume slider.

Mute the sound with the Ring/Silent switch on the side of your iPhone. (Mute is disabled in some countries/regions.)

Note: The camera shutter does not make a sound when the Live Photo icon is on.

How to Achieve Sharp Photo & Distinct Background in the Dark Surrounding

To overcome poor light or dark surroundings, Apple introduces a sophisticated Light Detection and Ranging (LiDAR) Scanner for Night Mode Portrait.

It has rapid autofocus in poor light to produce distinct background and cop-out the real images, and carry out next stage of Augmented Reality (AR).

It could be used to rearrange the position of the images on your portrait coverage.

When you press and hold any farther image, move it close to the other image(s) to remove in-between distance.

To prevent night defects on your photograph you have to make use of Night Mode Features that will completely remove shadow or reflection of darkness on your picture outcome.

Look at the top left side of the Camera interface you will see Flash and Night mode, when you tap on Flash automatically Night Mode will OFF but when you tap on Night Mode instantly Flash will go OFF.

When you hit on the Night Mode again it will disable the feature: More so, your iPhone will automatically show Night Mode to control the light around the image when the surrounding is dark.

How to Activate the Camera QR Code Scanner

1. Homescreen: Hit on the Settings icon.

2. Settings: Select Camera

3. Hit on the Scan QR Code activation switch to activate it. The switch will change from white to green.

4. Swipe Up to go back to Homescreen.

How You Can Use the Camera App to Scan the QR Code on Your iPhone

1. **Lock Screen or Homescreen or Control Center: Hit on the Camera icon Camera**

2. **Ensure that you are using the Rear (Back) Camera. If not, hit on the Camera turning icon (rotator) at the bottom right of the screen to turn the camera view to the rear Camera.**

3. **Position your camera to focus on the Quick Response Code.**

4. **A notification will show up on your screen for you to open the Website link (e.g. Open "amazon.com" in Safari).**

5. **Hit on the notification to open the website link with the Quick Response.**

How to Use High Dynamic Range (HDR) Camera to Produce Outstanding Photo Shoots

The use of High Dynamic Range (HDR) will make your pictures look more colorful, real, and attractive.

It could enable automatically or manually. When the camera is set to Auto HDR every photo shoot that will be taken will be automatically beautified with perfect color and awesome effect.

But if you disable Auto HDR, you will see the option of HDR at top of the

ViewFind for you to tap and select from the menu including Auto, On, and Off.

If you select the On option before you take any picture, you have to enable the manual function of the HDR effect on the picture.

When you select the Off option from the menu then you have disabled the function of HDR on every picture that you will be taken after.

But if you select the Auto option that means you have manually chosen Auto HDR which could be also off by tapping on the HDR menu at the top of the Viewfinder.

However, if you prefer having the HDR option to be permanently fixed to Auto HDR without showing the icon at the top menu, then you have to Settings to get it done.

1. **Homescreen: Hit on the icon Settings: Select Camera**
2. **Hit on the Auto HDR activation switch to change to green.**
3. **Swipe Up to go back to Homescreen**
4. **Launch your Camera by tapping on the Camera icon.**
5. **Start taking your pictures. All your pictures will be automatically enhanced with high dynamic range color effects and come out pretty good.**

How to Backup All the Saved Pictures with iCloud Photo Library

This will quickly save all your photos and video iCloud storage to prevent total loss when your iPhone is lost or suddenly develops a technical problem that may cause your iPhone to delete all the documents on it. But, since they have been saved in the iCloud Photo Library, you could recover all back on your iPhone completely.

1. Homescreen: Hit on the icon Settings: Select Photo
2. Hit on iCloud Photo Library activation switch to change to green.
3. Swipe up from the bottom center to return to Homescreen.
4. Homescreen: Press the Siri button and ask Siri: Hey Siri! Show me all Photos that were taken yesterday. Immediately, all the pictures you took yesterday will display for you to see on your screen.

How to Permit Siri to Search Photos on Your iPhone

When you enable Siri to always search for any particular photo for you on the iPhone, it will quickly provide all the requested Photos within a second.

1. Homescreen: Hit on the icon Settings: Select Photo
2. Hit on Siri & Search
3. Hit on Search & Siri Suggestions activation switch to change to green
4. On the same page of Photo you can activate the following options to improve easy accessibility:
   - iCloud Photo Sharing: This will create albums to share with other people or subscribe to other people's shared albums.
   - Summarize Photos: The Photos tab will show every photo in your library in all views. You can choose compact, summarized views for Collection and Year.
   - View Full HDR: It will automatically adjust the display to show the complete dynamic range of Photos.
   - Show Holiday Events: Under Memory, this will enable you to see the holiday events for your Home Country.

- **Automatic:** Under Transfer to MAC or PC, you can tap this option also to be checked in order to automatically transfer Photos and Video in a compatible format, or always transfer the original file without checking for compatibility. Select Keep Original.

Hint: Do not enable Cellular Data to download Photos or Videos, therefore, deactivate the activation switch of Cellular Data when you tap on it. This will save your cellular data from being used up quickly.

Always use a Wi-Fi network connection to download photos and videos by going to Control Center and select Wi-Fi Icon.

Chapter 17: Screenshots

How to Take Screenshot or Screen Recording

Screenshots are perfect for sharing moments from your favorite videos, high scores, social media conversations, and almost everything you see on your screen. Here's how to take screenshots:

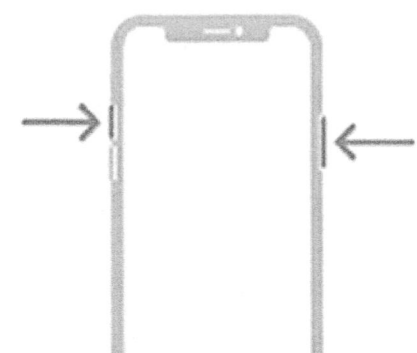

1. Open the screen you want to capture.
2. Simultaneously hold the Side button and the Up Volume button to capture.

Before taking screen records, you need to add the option to your Control Center in order to locate the controls easily. Use the steps below.

- Head to Settings, then to Control Center, and scroll to "Screen Recording."
- Tap the + (green plus) logo to add the screen recording controls to your "Control Center."

How to Make Screen Record

1. Swipe down from the upper-right corner of the screen and tap the "Screen Record" icon.
2. Wait 3 seconds before the recording starts. Your screen recording will start until you stop the recording.
3. To stop the screen recording, tap on the red status bar at the top, then tap stop. The video will automatically be stored in photos.

By default, there is no audio recording while you make a screen record. You can add audio along while you record the screen. Here is what to do to add audio:

1. Swipe down from the upper-right corner of your screen.
2. Hold the Screen Record icon, tap the microphone, and then tap start recording. The recording will work now with sound.
3. To stop recording, tap the red status bar on the top left of your screen.
4. Tap "Stop." The video will be stored in photos.

Not everything can be recorded. You can't record streaming apps like Netflix otherwise it would be possible to pirate their shows you are streaming. Although, you can record anything including game clips. You can't adjust screen recording settings and you cannot adjust the resolution or video quality of the clip.

1. Get to the screen that has the image or App you want to capture.
2. Set it the exact way you desire the shot to be or look like
3. Push the side button and home button simultaneously as shown below.

Viewing and Editing Screenshots

1. Launch the photos folder or App
2. Click on Albums
3. Click on Screenshots
4. Select Edit

Taking a Screenshot Using the Assistive Touch Capability of the iPhone 12

For users who may not be happy or comfortable with having to push two different buttons simultaneously to take a screenshot, it's possible to take a screenshot using just one simply to press the button. Here's how:

1. Go to Settings
2. Go to General
3. Select Accessibility
4. Enable the Assistive touch button (you will see a semi-transparent button added to the screen)
5. Click on the Customize Top Level Menu
6. Next, click on the custom icon (with one star) and select Screenshot from the list
7. To take a screenshot with the Assistive touch, click on the Assistive button and then tap the screenshot button.

You can replace the screenshot button with any of the default icons at any time you wish.

Chapter 18: Apple services (Apple Card, Apple Music, Apple iCloud, Apple TV...)

Setting Up Apple Pay

With Apple Pay, users can purchase items either online or in-store. All it would entail is just a touch of the Home button and a scan of your fingerprint; but before you can start using it, you have to set it up first. Here's how:

1. The first step is to add a card to Apple Pay
2. Open the Wallet app from the home screen display
3. Click on the +button on the top right side of the screen
4. Click on Continue or Next on the Apple Pay screen
5. Next, you have 2 options for entering the details of your credit or debit card. Either you manually input them or you scan with the phone camera (Should you decide to go with the camera scan option, make sure that the credit or debit card has embossed numbers because the photo detection system does not register flat numbers)
6. Click Next on the card details display screen
7. Input the expiration date and security code of the card manually
8. Click Next
9. Click Agree to accept the terms and conditions
10. Click Agree again
11. Select Next after you choose the verification method and tap Enter code.

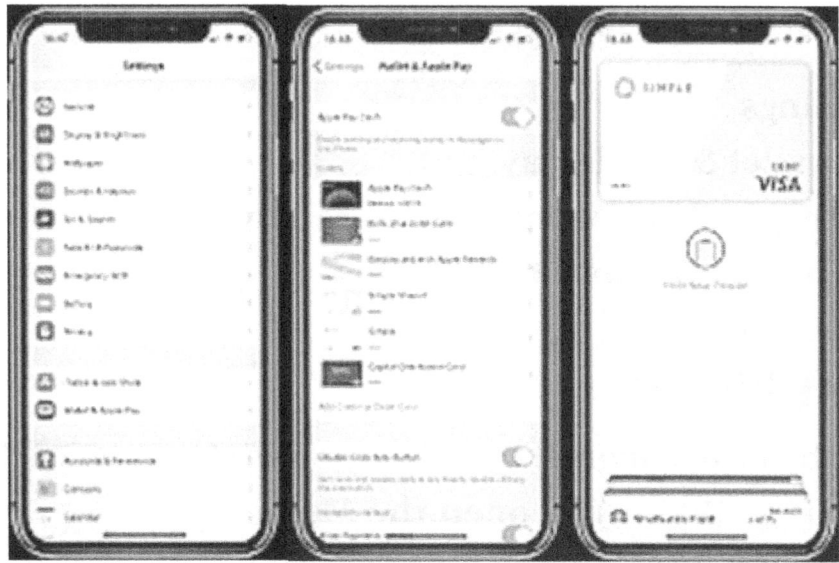

12. **Key in the verification code that was given to you. This could either be a text, call or email based on your chosen verification method.**

13. **Click on Next and then click on Done.**

Follow this same procedure in case you ever wish to add more debit or credit cards.

Changing the Initial Card for Apple Pay

The apple pay system allows you to register and effect payment for purchases and transactions using several credit and debit cards. You can seamlessly switch between them to make payments.

1. **Go to the Settings app on your device**
2. **Open Wallet & Apple pay**
3. **Click on the Default card**
4. **Select the card you would prefer to use as the standard for making purchases and transactions.**

Removing a Card from Apple Pay

1. Go to Settings
2. Click on wallet & Apple pay
3. Click on the card you would like to remove
4. Finally, click on Remove this card.

How to Play Music

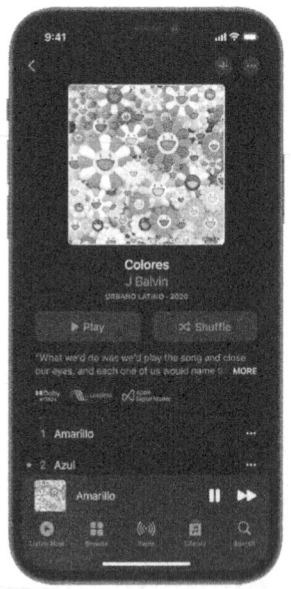

1. Click on the Music icon. This will open up the Library view. When you open the Music App the first time, you may see a screen telling you to sign up for Apple Music. You can ignore and dismiss this for now.
2. Enter the Library interface.
3. Choose from any of these options: Playlists, Artists, Albums, Songs, Genres, Compilations, and Downloaded Music. You will also see Recently Added.
4. Tap on Songs, here you will see all the tracks.

How to Subscribe to Apple Music

1. Go to iTunes or the Apple Music app. Or go to music.apple.com to subscribe.
2. Go to Listen Now or For You and tap the trial offer.
3. Choose a subscription (individual, family, or student). You can share your family subscription with six people.
4. Sign in with your Apple ID or create a new one if you don't have one.
5. Confirm your billing details and add a payment method.
6. Tap or click Join.

TV App

Install the Apple TV App on the iPhone

With the Apple TV application, you can watch Apple TV + firsts just as your other most loved shows, motion pictures, sports, and live news. Buy into Apple TV stations like CBS All Access and Showtime, watch titles from real-time features and link suppliers, and purchase or lease motion pictures and TV shows. The Apple TV ap-

plication is on your iPhone, iPad, iPod contact, Mac, Apple TV, and viable brilliant TVs and streaming gadgets so you can watch at home or any place you are.

Note: Availability of the Apple TV application and its highlights and admin-istrations, (for example, Apple TV +, Apple TV channels, sports, news, and upheld applications) fluctuate by nation or district.

Subscribe (Buy-in) to an Apple TV +

You can subscribe or buy into Apple TV + (not accessible in all nations/locales) and watch unique new Apple Originals without advertisements. Optionally, watch Apple TV + on iPhone, iPad, iPod touch, Mac, Apple TV, and compatible smart TVs and streaming devices, or download Apple Originals for offline viewing on iPhone, iPad, iPod touch, and Mac. If you use Family Sharing Up to five family members can share the subscription at no additional cost.

1. Touch Watch Now
2. Scroll down to the Apple TV + row, and do one of the following:
    - **Start Free Trial: Touch the button to begin your free trial (accessible for eligible Apple ID accounts). Apple TV + offers a**

free trial per subscriber or family.

- **Start a monthly subscription: Tap Subscribe.**

Review the subscription details, then confirm with your Face ID, Touch ID, or Apple ID.

Subscribe to Apple TV Channels

In the event that you buy into Apple TV channels, (for example, CBS All Access and Show Time), you can stream content without advertisements on request or download it for the disconnected survey. If you use Family Sharing, up to five family members can share the subscription at no additional cost.

1. Touch Watch now, then scroll down to browse available channels.
2. To watch a channel, do one of the following:
    - **Start Free Trial: Touch the button to begin your free trial (accessible for eligible Apple ID accounts). Each Apple TV channel offers a free trial per subscriber or family.**
    - **Start a monthly subscription: Tap Subscribe.**

Review the subscription details, then confirm with your Face ID, Touch ID, or Apple ID.

Include (Add) Your Cable or Satellite Service to the Apple TV App

Single sign-on provides instant access to all supported video applications in your subscription package.

1. Go to Settings> TV Provider.
2. Select your TV provider, then log in with your provider credentials.
3. If your TV provider is not listed, please log in directly from the

application you want to use.

Connect Compatible Apps to the Apple TV App

The Apple TV app recommends new content or the next episode of a show you're watching. The first time you play from a compatible application, touch Connect to allow connection to the Apple TV application.

Manage Your Connected App and Subscriptions

1. Touch View now, then touch the My Account button or your profile photo in the upper right.
2. Touch any of the following:
   - Connected apps: open or close apps. Linked apps appear in the Apple TV app on all devices that you signed in to with your Apple ID.
   - Manage subscriptions: Touch a subscription to change or cancel it.
   - Clear Playback History: Delete your viewing history from all Apple devices.

Books/Audiobooks

Discover and Purchase Books/Audiobooks in Apple Books App on iPhone

After selecting a book or audiobook, you can read or listen to it directly in the app.

1. Open Books and tap Library or Audiobooks to search for titles or tap Search to search for a specific title or author.
2. Tap a book cover to see more details, read a pre-

view, hear a preview, or mark if I want to read.

3. Tap Buy to purchase a title or tap Download to download a free title.

All buys are made with the installment technique related to your Apple ID.

Note: You can have books and audiobooks downloaded automatically over your mobile network when you are not connected to a Wi-Fi network. Go to Settings> Books, scroll down to Mobile data, tap Downloads and then Always allow.

Look Through (Read) Books in the Books App on iPhone

In the Books application, utilize the Reading Now and Library tabs at the lower part of the screen to see the books you are perusing, the books you need to peruse, your book assortments, and more.

- **Reading Now: Tap to access the books and audiobooks you are currently reading. Scroll down to see the books and audiobooks you've added to your Want to Read collection and the books you've tried. You can also set daily reading goals and track which books you have completed throughout the year.**
- **Library: Tap to view all the books, audiobooks, series, and PDF files that you have obtained from the library or manually added to your library. You can touch Collections to view your** books arranged in collections such as I want to read, My samples, Audiobooks, and Completed.

Listen to Audiobooks in Books App on iPhone

Utilize the Books app to listen to audiobooks on your iPhone.

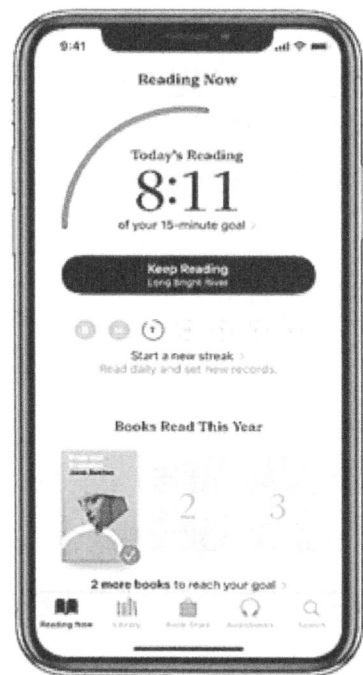

The audiobook player screen above shows the audiobook cover in the top center. Below the cover is the tracking number, the name of the audiobook, and the author. Below the audiobook's name is the player, and below are the play, pause, and rewind, and forward controls. Below the player controls is the volume slider. At the bottom of the screen, from left to right, you will find the Playback Speed, Sleep Timer, Playback Destination, and Track List buttons. The Library button is in the upper left corner.

Play an Audiobook

In Reading Now or your library's audiobook collection, tap the cover of the audiobook, and then do one of the following:

- **Forward or Rewind: Press and hold the rounded arrows, slide and hold the book cover, or use external controls such as headphones or car controls.**
- **Speed up or slow down: Touch the playback speed in the lower-left corner pick an alternate speed.**
- **Set a sleep timer: tap the sleep button and choose the duration.**
- **Go to a chapter: Tap the Table of Contents button, then tap a chapter.**

Note: some audiobooks refer to chapters as tracks or do not define chapters.

- **Go to a specific time: Drag the playhead directly under the cover of the audiobook. The point where you began listening is**

> marked with a gray circle on the outline. Tap the circle to go back to that place.

If there is no Wi-Fi internet connection available, the audiobooks will play through your provider's cellular network, which may incur additional charges. Audiobooks larger than 200MB cannot be streamed over a cellular network (iOS 13.3 or earlier).

AirPods

If you are watching a movie on your iPad, for example, and then want to listen to music or take a call on your phone, your AirPods will switch automatically.

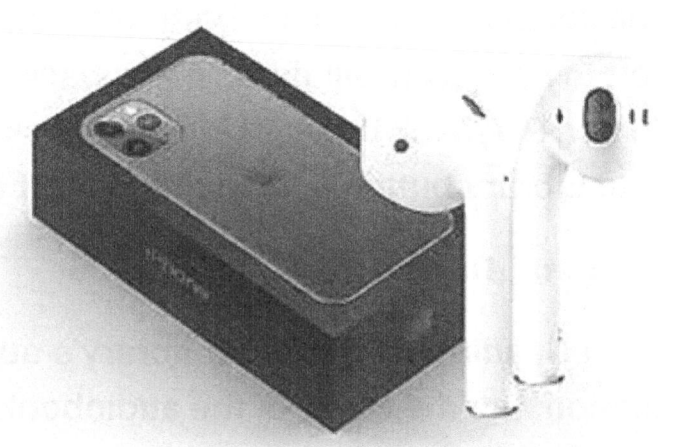

Spatial Audio

Apple also added spatial audio, which allows for dynamic head tracking of movies that make it sound like it's coming right from the device. When you turn your head, it knows that you've turned your head, and you can hear out of the side of the ear that is close to the screen. If you turn your head to the right and your left ear is close to the screen, it will sound as though you're standing in front of your display.

It will work with Apple TV and iPhone, iPad, and Mac in the future with MacOS Big Sur.

Your device will also let you know if you need to charge your AirPods and apple watch.

How to Use the Calculator on the iPhone 12

In the Calculator application, you can perform basic arithmetic calculations with the standard calculator. Or on the other hand utilize the scientific calculator for logarithmic, trigonometric functions, and exponential.

Ask Siri. Say something like, "What's 74 times 9?" or "What is 18% of 225?"

Use the Scientific Calculator

1. **Rotate iPhone to landscape view.**
2. **Copy, delete, or delete numbers**
   - **To copy a calculation result: Touch and hold the calculation result on the screen, tap Copy, then paste the result elsewhere, such as a note or message.**
   - **Delete the last digit: If you make a mistake while entering a number, swipe left or right on the top screen.**
   - **Clear the screen: touch the clear button (C) to clear the last entry or touch the clear all button (AC) to clear all entries.**

Chapter 19: How to Activate Siri

Siri is apple's own virtual assistant and can be an invaluable tool. It can perform various tasks tailored to your prompts and convenience, Siri can help you translate, set timers, announce weather conditions and so much more.

Setting Up Siri

1. Go to settings > Siri and Search.
2. Turn on listening for 'hey Siri'
3. Turn on press side button for Siri (if you want to summon Siri with a button).

Make Sure Siri Is Enabled on iPhone

If Siri isn't enabled on your iPhone, go to Settings> Siri & Search, then open one of the following options:

- Press the side button for Siri (on an iPhone with Face ID)
- Press Home for Siri (on other iPhone models)

Summoning Siri

To summon Siri, say 'Hey Siri' or press the appropriate summoning button depending on your settings.

Go ahead to ask Siri a question or give a prompt.

Response from Siri

Tap to continue speaking to Siri.

How to Add Siri

How to perform a Siri query in iOS 14

If you enabled verbal triggers, start by stating "Hey Siri" followed by your question.

You can also hold down the Side button, the Home Button, or in some iPad Pro models, the Top button, followed by your query.

Siri will automatically respond or perform the task once the query is made.

You can extend Siri's time if the timing out is too early. Simply hold the Side, Top, or Home button during the query. Release the button when you are done.

How to Adjust Siri

1. Go to Settings and then to Siri and Search.
2. Make the necessary changes to Siri and then exit Settings.

Discover What Siri Can Do on iPhone

Use Siri on iPhone for information and tasks. Siri and her response appear in addition to what you're doing and allow you to see information on the screen.

Siri is interactive. At the point when Siri shows a web interface, you can tap it to see more data in your default internet browser. When Siri's onscreen response includes buttons or controls, you can tap them to perform more actions. Also, you can contact Siri again to pose another inquiry or do an extra undertaking for you.

- Find answers to your questions: search the web for information, get sports scores, get arithmetic, and more. "Hey, Siri, what causes a rainbow?" "Hey Siri, what was the Orioles game score yesterday?" Or "Hey Siri, what is the derivative of cosine x?" Say something like.

- Perform tasks with applications on iPhone: use Siri to control applications with your voice. For example, say something like "Hello Siri, schedule a meeting with Gordon at 9 o'clock" to create an event in Calendar, or something like "Hello Siri, add pumpkin and onions to my shopping list.

- Send and reply to a message: Say something like "Hello Siri, send Eliza a message about tomorrow" or "Hello Siri, reply to this great news." You can even use Siri to send voice messages. If you connect your AirPods (AirPods Pro and 2nd generation AirPods) to your iPhone and a message arrives, Siri can read the message to you even if your iPhone is locked. Siri listens to messages after reading them so you can reply without saying "Hello Siri." See Use Siri on iPhone with AirPods.

- Translate Languages: "Hello Siri, how do you say thank you in Mandarin?"

How to Use Siri in Your Car

If you've never used CarPlay, you need to pair the two devices first. So, connect your phone to the car. If wireless CarPlay is available, hold down the voice button on your steering wheel to launch the configuration. Then on your device:

1. Head to Settings and tap your car's name
2. Then go to General and then to CarPlay. That's it!

Call Siri with a Button

When you invoke Siri with a button, Siri responds loudly when the iPhone is in ring mode and silent when the iPhone is in silent mode. See put iPhone in ringer or silent mode. To change this, see Change the way Siri responds.

Do one of the following:

- **On an iPhone with Face ID: press-hold the side button.**
- **Press-hold the home button on an iPhone with a home button.**
- **EarPods: Press and hold the center or search button.**
- **CarPlay: Press-hold the voice command button on the guiding wheel or the CarPlay home screen, touch and hold the main button.**
- **Siri Eyes Free: Press and hold the voice command button on the steering wheel.**

When Siri appears, ask Siri a question or ask her to do a task for you.

For example, "What is 18 percent of 225?" Say something like that.

Touch the Listen button to ask Siri another question or perform another task.

You can also summon Siri by holding down or double-tapping the AirPods.

Ask Siri on iPhone

Speaking to Siri is a fast way to get things done. Ask Siri to translate a sentence, set a timer, search for a location, report the weather, and more. If you use Siri the more, the better it understands what you need.

To use Siri, the iPhone must be connected to the Internet. Mobile phone charges may apply.

How to Enable Siri and Screen Time on iPhone 12

The next screen will allow you to choose if you want to activate Siri. You also want to enable Siri. Siri is a vital tool to have at your beck and call. With Siri you can ask your iPhone questions, set timers, send messages and have it read emails, and even answer text messages and make calls.

The last big setup screen is for Screen Time. This allows you to track your iPhone and show how much you use it in different applications. It is a powerful tool, so it is good to activate it.

Finally, tap "Get Started" and you will be taken to the iPhone 12 home screen. Congratulations! Your iPhone is now ready to use!

Shortcut for Siri

Now let's talk about a shortcut to access Siri, Apple's virtual assistant for the iPhone and other Apple-made devices. To summon Siri, all you have to do is press and hold on the side button (also known as the power button), and Siri automatically comes on. You can also summon Siri by simply saying, "Hey Siri," and Siri will become active almost instantly.

Here's how you can access your Lock Screen. The way to access your Lock Screen is to swipe down from the top-left side of your display.

Chapter 20: How to Set Screen Time

One major novelty of iPhone 12 is the inclusion of Screen Time, a new section in the Settings App that will allow you to manage the time you use your iPhone, and also know in detail everything you do with it.

It is a bit ironic that Apple makes an effort to make us use the iPhone less, but actually, Screen Time all it does is provide information and allow us to receive a series of notifications as a warning when we exceed the usage limits that we have configured.

In other words, if you do not want anything to burden you in terms of the hours you use the iPhone, you can disable all notifications, which arrive in the form of local notifications.

How to Enable Screen Time on iPhone 12

By default, Screen Time is enabled in iOS 12. If for some reason Screen Time is disabled on your device, here is how to enable it:

1. Go to the home screen of your device and open Settings.
2. Once you're in Settings, tap the Screen Time settings.
3. On the Screen Time page, activate the Screen Time option.
4. The next screen shows what Screen Time is about. You can read the information on the screen to learn more about the function.
5. After that, tap the Continue button to move to the next page.
6. Confirm whether the iPhone is yours or your child's. For this example, tap the This is my iPhone button. You have just activated Screen Time on your iPhone!

How to Use Screen Time

Now that you have enabled Screen Time on your device, learn how to use and maximize the feature:

Open Screen Time from your phone's settings. There is no separate app for Screen Time. This feature is only accessible through your phone settings.

- View your phone usage.
- Schedule to downtime
- Set application limits.
- Whitelist applications.
- Block content.
- Use a Screen Time password lock.
- Set screen time for the family.

Screen Time is a tool that helps you monitor time spent on apps and websites with the iPhone. With this, you have insights into your usage trends and can then put in place controls and limits to regulate the time spent using specific activities and view reports for you or your children. Screen Time does the following:

- Compute time spend using different categories of apps
- Time spent using each time daily
- Details of apps you used beyond the limit you have set
- The number of times you pick up your device and the apps you use.

Set App Limits

Settings > Screen Time > App limits > Add limit > Select the app categories > Set the amount of time > Add.

Choose apps You Want to Use Always

Settings > Screen Time > Always Allowed > add the app to the 'Allowed apps' list.

- **Turn on screen time: You can turn on screen time by selecting Settings > Screen Time > Turn On 'Screen Time' > Continue > This is my iPhone. Next, you can Share across devices if you want Screen Time reports to include time spent on other devices with the same Apple ID signed in and Use Screen Time Passcode to put an additional level of security on access to the Screen Time settings (to request for a password to allow additional time when the time limit has passed).**
- **Some content may not be suitable for certain ages of users. To restrict access to this type of content in iTunes and App Store, Settings > Screen Time > Content& Privacy restrictions > Turn on Content and Privacy restrictions > Options. Here you can set content allowances for iTunes store and App store purchases, app usage, and content ratings.**
- **Set limits and restrictions: You can use downtime (time away from the screen), App Limits (set limits for the amount of time spent in specific apps, types of apps, and websites), and Apps that are always allowed (even during scheduled Downtimes).**

Arrange the Brightness and Color of the iPhone Screen

On an iPhone, you can dim the screen to extend battery life, use the Night Shift function, set the dark mode, and adjust the screen automatically according to your lighting conditions.

Turn Dark Mode On or Off

The dark mode gives the entire iPhone experience a dark color scheme that is perfect in low-light conditions. You can choose to turn on dark mode from the control center or set it to turn on automatically at night (or on a custom schedule) in Settings. When Dark Mode is on, for example, you can use the iPhone while reading in bed without disturbing the person next to you.

Do one of the following:

- **Open the Control Center, press and hold the Brightness button, and then press the Appearance button to turn dark mode on or off.**
- **Select Settings> Display and brightness, select Dark to turn on dark mode or Light to turn it off.**

Set Dark Mode to Turn On and Off Automatically

1. **Select Settings> Display and brightness.**
2. **Turn on Automatic, and then tap Options.**

Select Sunset to Sunrise or Custom Schedule

If you select a Custom plan, press the plan to plan when dark mode is on or off.

If you select Sunset and Sunrise, iPhone uses your clock and geographic location to determine when it's night.

Adjust the Screen Brightness Manually

To make the iPhone screen brighter, do one of the following:

- **Open the control center and drag the brightness button.**
- **Select Settings> Display and brightness, and then drag the slid-**

er.

Adjust the Screen Brightness Automatically

The iPhone uses the built-in ambient light sensor to adjust the screen brightness for current lighting conditions.

1. Go to Settings> Availability.
2. Touch Screen and Text Size, then turn on Auto-Brightness.

Turn True Tone On or Off

On supported models, turn on the True Tone feature to automatically adjust the color and intensity of the screen to the ambient light.

Do one of the following:

- Open the Control Center, press and hold the brightness button, and then press the True Tone button to turn True Tone on or off.
- Go to Settings> Display and brightness, then turn the real sound on or off.

Turn Night Shift on or off

You can also turn on Night Shift manually, which is useful if you are in a dark room during the day.

1. Open the Control Center, press and hold Brightness, and then press Night Shift.
2. Set night shift for automatic on and off

Night Shift allows you to move the screen colors to the warmer end of the spectrum at night and make it easier to see the screen in your eyes.

Turn on Scheduled

To adjust the Night Shift color balance, drag the slider below the color temperature toward the warmer or cooler end of the spectrum.

Tap Off, then select Sunset to Sunrise or Custom Plan.

- If you select Custom Schedule, press the options to schedule Night Shift on and off.
- If you select Sunset and Sunrise, iPhone uses your clock and geographic location to determine when it's night.

Note: Sunset to Sunrise is not available if you have turned off Location Services in Settings> Privacy, or if you have turned off the time zone setting in Settings> Privacy> Location Services> System Services.

Chapter 21: Control Center

The Control Center is the window that appears in iOS when you slide your finger from any screen from bottom to top... This section serves as a shortcut panel to access the most popular tools on your iPhone 12. The primary functions of the Control Center are the following:

- Activate airplane mode.
- Activate a wireless connection.
- Activate Bluetooth.
- Control music playback.
- Activate/Deactivate automatic screen rotation. Active "Do Not Disturb" mode.
- Control screen brightness.

How to Access Control Center on iPhone 12 and 12 Pro

Since the multitasking easy app switcher is now invoked by a swipe up, the Control Center had to be from the bottom to the top. And the switch to the top of the Control Center meant that the Notification Center had to learn to share. Notification Center is therefore now limited to swiping down from the "horn" at the top left or the TrueDepth camera module in the center. And the Control Center, as the new home, gets the right horn.

1. Touch the right "horn" with your finger (where the battery and cell signal indicator are).
2. Swipe down.

Again, for Control Center entry, you can also swipe down from the top right of Reachability.

Access a Paired Bluetooth Device from the Control Center

1. Go to the Control Center.
2. Long press the network settings card from the top-left side of the screen with four icons
3. Click on the Bluetooth icon. The available device options; from either iPhone or other accessible Bluetooth devices will be depicted.
4. Look for the inscription of the Bluetooth device you intend to switch to on the list and click on the device's name.

Connect to Wi-Fi Through the Control Center

1. Open the Control Center.
2. Long press the four-icon panel (including Airplane Mode, Mobile Data, Wi-Fi, and Bluetooth buttons) located at the top-left corner to expand it.
3. At this point, long press on the Wi-Fi icon. A secondary screen will now appear listing the Wi-Fi networks in range. The Wi-Fi network you are connected to will be at the top of the list.

To change networks, click on the inscription of the desired network.

The Connectivity Panel

In the top left corner of the Control Center, there is a small square containing four icons, namely:

- Airplane mode

- **Cellular Connection Strength**
- **Wi-Fi**
- **Bluetooth**

The connectivity and signal strength is right at the top left edge of the Control Center. Here, the name of the Cell Phone Carrier is displayed along with the Cellular Connection Strength. Whenever you connect to Wi-Fi, the signal strength of the Wi-Fi connection is also displayed here.

At the Control Center's top-right edge, the Do Not Disturb icon, along with the Bluetooth, battery icon, and battery percentage, are all displayed.

Media Control

The square box right under the battery icon is a control panel responsible for controlling running media files. If you're listening to an audio file, this square box in the control panel lets you pause, play, forward, and rewind the running audio file without having to leave the Control Center. It is an easy-access control panel for whatever app you're using that uses media functionality.

Portrait Orientation Lock

The Portrait Orientation Lock, which sits just below the square box containing the connectivity icons, is responsible for locking your iPhone in portrait mode or permitting autorotation. When Portrait Orientation Lock is on, you can only use the iPhone in portrait mode. However, when off, you can use the iPhone in both portrait and landscape modes. The lock is turned on and off by simply tapping on the Portrait Orientation Lock icon.

Do Not Disturb

Right next to the Portrait Orientation Lock is the Do Not Disturb icon. This feature helps to turn off all sounds from incoming phone calls, alerts, and notifications when you lock your iPhone. You can schedule Do Not Disturb to work at certain times and only permit calls from particular contacts. You can turn this feature on and off by simply tapping on the icon in the Control Center. This feature is helpful when you're in meetings, driving, taking classes, and in circumstances where you want no distraction.

Brightness and Volume touch controls

Sitting beside the Do Not Disturb icon are the Brightness and Volume touch controls. With these two controls, you can adjust the display brightness and phone volume, respectively. Suppose you 3D-touch on the Brightness controls (which is to press a little bit harder). In that case, you can also turn on True Tone, which automatically adjusts your display brightness and color temperature based on the ambient light condition of its immediate surroundings to give your display a natural feel. You can also turn on Night Shift, which helps protect your eyes from excessive light exposure from your device at night. You can schedule the Night Shift feature to take effect at particular times every day.

Screen Mirroring

There is also the Screen Mirroring icon below the Portrait Orientation Lock on the Do Not Disturb icons. This icon controls the Screen Mirroring feature, which allows you to mirror the screen of your iPhone on another device such as a Macintosh or PC, TVs that support this feature, etc.

Flashlight, Timer & Calculator

There is also the Flashlight icon, which turns the rear camera flash on and off when touched. Next to the Flashlight icon is the Timer, which works like a stopwatch. Next is the Timer is the Calculator, which you can use to make mathematical calculations. Next to the Calculator is the Camera icon, which launches the Camera app immediately you tap on it.

Chapter 22: How to Manage Events in Your iPhone 12

Make and Modify Events in Calendar on iPhone

Utilize the Calendar application to make and modify meetings, events, and appointments.

A calendar in day view showing the events of the day. Touch the Calendars button at the bottom of the screen to change calendar accounts. Touch the Inbox button at the bottom right to view invitations.

Ask Siri. Say something like:

- Make an interview with John at 11 am.
- Do I have a meeting at 8 am?
- Where is my 3:30 meeting?

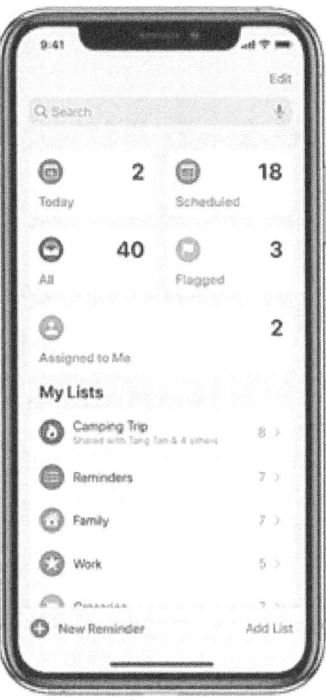

Add an Event

1. In day view, tap the Add button in the upper left.
2. Fill in the appointment details.
3. Enter the title and location of the event, the start and end times, how often it will repeat, etc.
4. Touch Add.

Add a Warning

You can set up an alert so that you are reminded of an event in advance.

1. Touch the event, then touch Edit in the upper right corner.
2. In the event details, tap Alert.
3. Choose when you want to receive a reminder. For example: At the time of the occasion, 5 minutes before or another option.

Note: When you add the address of the event location, Calendar uses Apple Maps to find locations, traffic, and transit options to let you know when it's time to leave.

Add an Attachment

You can add an attachment to a calendar event to share with guests.

1. Touch the event, then touch Edit in the upper right corner.
2. In the appointment details, tap Add attachment. The Files application opens and displays recently opened files.
3. Look for the file or document you intend to attach.
4. To find the file, enter its name in the search field, scroll, touch folders to open them, touch Browse to find other locations (such as iCloud Drive), and more.
5. Touch Done.
6. To erase the attachment, touch the event, tap Edit in the top right corner, slide left on the attachment, and then tap Delete.

Search for Events in Other Apps

Siri can propose occasions found in Mail, Messages, and Safari, for example, flight reservations and inn reservations, so you can undoubtedly add them to Calendar.

1. Proceed to Settings. Then to Calendar> Siri & Search.
2. Enable Show Siri Suggestions in App to allow Siri to suggest events in other apps.

3. Turn on **Learn from this app** to allow Siri to suggest suggestions in other apps based on your use of Calendar.

Edit an Event

You can change the time of an event and all other event details.

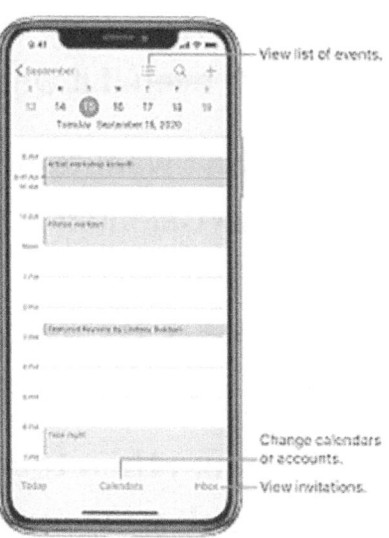

- **Change the time: In day view, contact and hold the occasion and drag it to another time or change the capture points.**
- **Edit event details: touch the event, touch Edit at the top right, then in the event details touch a setting to change it or touch a field to enter new information.**

Delete an Event

In day view, touch the event, then touch Delete event at the bottom of the screen

Mail and Obtain Invitations in Calendar on iPhone

Mail (send) and obtain (receive) invitations to meetings and events in the Calendar app. Microsoft Exchange, iCloud, and some CalDAV servers permit you to send or mail and obtain meeting invitations. (Not all calendar servers support all features).

Invite Others to an Event

1. **Touch the event, touch Edit, touch Guests, and then touch Add attendees. Or, if you haven't scheduled the event, tap it, tap**

Guests, and then tap the Email Invitees button.

2. Enter the names or email addresses of the invitees or touch the Add button to select Contacts.

3. Touch Done (or touch Send if you haven't scheduled the event).

Microsoft Exchange and some other servers allow you to invite people to an event, even if it wasn't you who planned it.

If you don't want to be notified when someone declines a meeting, go to Settings> Calendar and uncheck Show declined invitees.

Respond to an Event Invitation

1. Touch an event notification to reply to it. Or, in Calendar, touch Inbox, then touch an invitation.

2. Touch your answer: accept, maybe, or reject.

3. To reply to an email invitation, touch the underlined text in the email, and then touch Show in the calendar.

To view declined events, tap Calendars at the bottom of the screen and turn on Show declined events.

Plan an Event without Blocking Your Schedule

You can add an event to your calendar without displaying the busy period for other people who send you invitations.

1. Touch the event, then touch Edit.

2. Touch View as, then touch Free.

Suggest a Different Meeting Time

You can propose a different time for a meeting invitation that you have received.

1. Tap the meeting> Propose new time.
2. Tap the time and enter a new one.

Contingent upon the capacities of your schedule worker, the coordinator will get a counter proposition or an email with your recommendation.

E-mail Visitors Quickly

1. Touch an occasion that has attendees.
2. Tap Guests, then tap the Send email to invitees button.

Change the Way You View Events in Calendar on iPhone

In the Calendar application, you can see a day, seven days, a month, or a year at a time, or view a rundown of forthcoming occasions. To change the calendar view, do one of the following:

- Zoom in or out: touch a year, month, or day to zoom in or out on your calendar. Pinch in the week or day view to zoom in or out.
- View a weekly calendar: Turn iPhone sideways in Day view.
- View a list of events: In Month view, tap the List button to view the events for the day. (Tap the list button again to return to the month view.)

Customize Your Calendar On iPhone

In the Calendar application, you can pick which day of the week the schedule begins with, see numbers for the week, pick elective schedules (for instance, to show dates in Chinese or Hebrew), override the automatic time zone, and more.

1. Proceed to Settings> Calendar.
2. Then, make a choice of the settings and highlights you want.

Track Events in Calendar on iPhone

In the Calendar app, you can customize notifications that notify you of upcoming calendar events, invites, and more. You can likewise ensure your occasions and other schedule data is stayed up with the latest on the entirety of your gadgets.

Customize Calendar

1. Go to Settings> Notifications> Calendar.
2. Turn on Allow notifications.
3. Tap an event type (for example Upcoming Events), then choose how and where you want to display notifications for those events, for example on the lock screen, in the notice Center, as posters at the peak of the screen, with a warning sound, etc.

Keep Your Calendar Current on All Your Gadgets

You can use iCloud to keep your calendar information up to date on any of your devices that are signed in with the same Apple ID.

Proceed to Settings. Then input [your name]> iCloud and activate Calendars.

If you don't want to use iCloud for your calendar, you can sync your calendar data between your iPhone and your computer.

Chapter 23: How to Change the Wallpaper

On the iPhone, select a photo or image as the background for the lock screen or the home screen. You can choose between dynamic and still images.

With the background settings screen, a new background selection button at the top, and images of the screen lock and home screen with the current background.

Change Background

Select Settings> Wallpaper> Select New Wallpaper.

Do one of the following:

- **Select a preset image from the group at the top of the screen (Dynamic, Snapshots, etc.). The background marked with the Appearance button changes its appearance when dark mode is on.**
- **Select your photo (tap the album, then tap the photo).**

To place the selected image, pinch it to zoom in, then use your finger to move the image. Tighten the clip to zoom out.

Press the Parallax Effect button to turn on Perspective Zoom (available with some background selections), which moves the background as if you changed the viewpoint. The perspective zoom option does not appear when motion reduction is turned on (in Settings> Accessibility> Motion).

Stop the Movement of Screen Elements on the iPhone

Press Setup, and then select one of the following:

- Set the screen lock
- Set the home screen
- Set up both

To turn on Perspective Zoom for already set wallpapers, go to Settings> Wallpaper, tap Lock screen or Home screen, and then tap Perspective zoom.

Set a Live Photo as the background for the lock screen

1. To set Live Photo as wallpaper, press and hold the lock screen to play Live Photo - on all iPhone models except iPhone SE (Generation 1).
2. Select Settings> Wallpaper> Select New Wallpaper.
3. Do one of the following:
   - Tap Live, then select Live Photo.
   - Tap the Live Photos album, then select a Live photo (you may have to wait for the download).
   - Tap Layout, and then select Display Layout or Both.

How to Adjust Wallpaper

Wallpapers are a perfect way to add some personality and customization to your phone. And while your images can still be used as wallpapers. It's easy to change your wallpaper, you just need to select the right picture!

Go to Settings, then to Wallpaper, and then tap on Choose a New Wallpaper. You can choose from Apple's stock images or from your image library.

Tap the style of wallpaper you wish to use:

- **Dynamic: Choose this is for Apple's stock images with effects that fade into view and react to your phone's movement.**
- **Still: For still images.**
- **Live: For a Live Photo that will animate after a firm press**
- **Photo Library: An image or live photo from your photo library.**

Select your new wallpaper to enter the Preview mode. In Preview mode, you can choose how to show your image. Tap any of the following options:

- **Still: The chosen still image will be displayed as your wallpaper.**
- **Perspective: As you move the screen, the still image will change the perspective slightly. (Don't use this if you're prone to motion sickness.)**
- **Live Photo: If you chose a Live Photo image, this option allows you to animate the image after a firm press.**

Tap Set.

Tap any of the following option: Set Lock Screen, Set Home Screen or both.

How to Change the Wallpaper Directly from the Photos App

1. Go to "Photos" and select an image.
2. Tap on the Share button. Find Use as Wallpaper and select it to enter the Preview mode.
3. Position the image and zoom it in accordingly.
4. Select any of the following options:
   - Still: The chosen still image will be displayed.

- **Perspective:** As you move the screen, the still image will change the perspective slightly. (Don't use this if you're prone to motion sickness.)
- **Live Photo:** If you chose a Live Photo image, the image will animate after a firm press.

Tap Set.

Tap any of the following option: Set Lock Screen, Set Home Screen or both.

Chapter 24: Move Home Screen Apps

How You Could Rearrange App's Icons on the Home Screen

Apps could be moved from one place to another place on your iPhone Home screen. You may choose to rearrange the apps in alphabetical order or base on how you will be using them regularly or how they will be more convenient for you.

1. Home screen: For a short time press hold the screen for an optional dialog box to appear.

2. Optional Dialog Box: Hit on the Rearrange Apps option. Immediate the entire apps will be shaking and unstable with the Cancel sign attached to the left top angle of each app.

3. Apps: Place your hand on each App you wanted to move and drag the app to the favorite place. As soon as, you are through with the rearranging of the Apps as you wanted then Swipe Up the screen from the bottom.

How You Can Keep Many Apps in a Customized File on Homescreen

1. Homescreen: For a short time press the screen for a dialog box

to come up.

2. **Dialog Box:** Hit on the Rearrange Apps option. Immediate the entire apps will be stirring and unstable with the Cancel sign attached to the left top angle of each app.

3. **Apps:** Position your hand on an App and drag it to another app you want to keep in the same file. Before you release the dragged App on the below App make sure that a transparent white square shape appears around the below app. You will see the File Name text field above, hit on the text field to name the file.

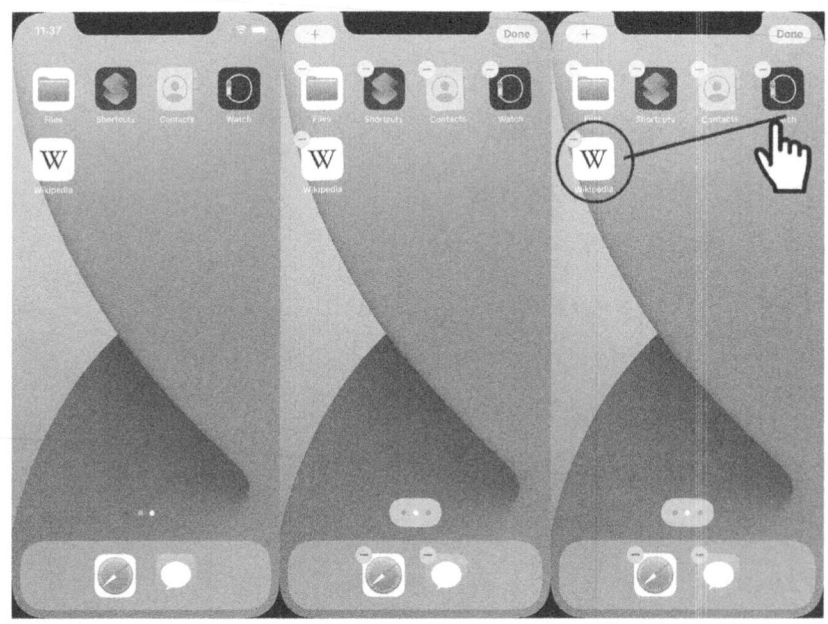

If you want more than 2 Apps in a file, then continue dragging Apps on the file you have created and hit on the outer part of the file to restore and fix it.

As soon as, you are through with the rearrangement of the Apps as you wanted then Swipe Up the screen from the bottom, the whole apps will come back to normal.

How You Can Delete Apps on the Homescreen

1. Hold down the app until you will see an optional dialog box.
2. Hit on the Delete option. Immediately the app will be removed.

Or

1. Hold down the app till you will see the whole app stirring and unstable with the Remove sign at the left angle of the apps.
2. Hit on the Remove sign. Immediately the app will be removed from the page and the whole apps will automatically rearrange itself.
3. Swipe Up to stabilize and normalize the apps.

Open Applications from the Home Screen

1. To access the home screen, swipe up from the bottom of the screen (on an iPhone with Face ID)
2. Swipe left or right to find apps on other pages of the home screen.
3. To open an application, touch the corresponding icon.
4. To return to the first page of the home screen, swipe up from the bottom of the screen (on an iPhone with facial recognition). It is also possible to move apps, organize apps or delete apps (Explore the app library).

The App Library automatically classifies your apps into categories like creative, social, entertainment, etc.

The apps you use the most are at the top of the screen and at the top level of their categories so you can easily find and open them.

To find the app library:

1. Go to the home screen
2. Swipe left across all the pages on your home screen. In the application library, you can do the following:
   - Open the app: Tap the app if it's visible.
   - Expand category: If there are more applications below the top level in a category (indicated by some small application icons), touch the small icons to display all applications in the category.
   - Search apps: Touch the search box at the top of the screen to see your apps in alphabetical order. Enter the name of an app in the search box to find it.
   - Take quick actions: Long-press an app to open a menu of quick actions.

NOTE: If you hold down an app for too long before choosing a quick action, all the apps will start to wobble. Tap Done (on an iPhone with facial recognition).

Add an App to the Home Screen

Touch and hold the app to open a quick action menu, then select Add to home screen (only available if the app is not already on the home screen). The application will continue to appear in the application library.

Chapter 25: Using Airdrop

Airdrop enables you to send and receive documents, photos, map locations, files, and webpages wirelessly (Wi-Fi and Bluetooth) to a nearby Mac, iPhone, or iPad.

Share Files Via Airdrop

- Just click on the item you want to send, select the Share > Airdrop and then the profile picture of a nearby Airdrop user.
- From the Finder app, click Airdrop and drag the file to the recipients' device. The recipient has to choose whether or not to accept the file for the share to be completed.

Receive Files Via Airdrop

1. Ensure that in the AirDrop window, you have set 'Allow me to be discovered by' and choose the appropriate option (no one, contacts, or everyone) in Control Center.
2. Navigate to the Airdrop notification and click Accept from the pop-up menu. The file received will be added to the Downloads folder by default.

Airdrop works over Bluetooth and as such, the Bluetooth of both devices must be turned on and within 30 feet (9 meters) of each other.

Before You Begin

- Make sure the person you are sending is nearby, within range of Bluetooth and Wi-Fi.

- Make sure you and the person you are sending are turned on via Wi-Fi and Bluetooth. If Personal Hotspot is turned on for any of you, turn it off.

- Make sure the person you are sending is set to receive AirDrop only from Contacts. In that case, and you are in contact, you must enter the email address or mobile number in the contact to use AirDrop.

- If you are not in contact, set the AirDrop receiver to All to receive the file.

- You can set the AirDrop Receive setting to Connections Only or Off at any time to control who can see your device and send content in AirDrop.

Using AirDrop

1. Open the app, press Share. When you share a photo from Photos, you can swipe left or right and select multiple photos.

2. Touch the AirDrop user you want to share with. Or you can use AirDrop on your own Apple devices. Do not see the AirDrop user or the other device? Find out what you need to do.

If the person you are sharing with is in your contacts, a picture with your name will be displayed. If they are not in contact, you will only see their names without a picture.

How to Accept AirDrop

When someone shares something with you using AirDrop, a preview alert is displayed. Press Accept or Reject.

If you click Accept, AirDrop will go through the same app you sent it from. For example, photos appear in Photos, and websites open in Safari. Application links open in the App Store, so you can download or purchase the app.

If you give yourself an AirDrop, such as a photo from iPhone to Mac, you will not see the Accept or Reject option - it will be automatically sent to your device. Just make sure both devices are signed in with the same Apple ID

Change AirDrop settings

To choose who can see your device and send content in AirDrop:

1. Go to Settings, tap General.
2. Press AirDrop, then select an option.

You can also adjust AirDrop settings in Control Center. This is how:

1. On an iPhone X or later, or an iPad or iPad running iOS 12 or later, slide your finger down from the upper right corner of the screen to open the Control Center. On the iPhone 8 or later, slide your finger up from the bottom of the screen.
2. Press or hold the Network Settings tab at the top left.
3. Press and hold the AirDrop button and select one of the following options:
   - Off: You will not receive AirDrop requests.
   - Contacts only: Only contacts can see your device.
   - Everyone: All nearby Apple devices using AirDrop can see your device.

If you see the payout option and it does not affect your change:

1. Select Settings> Screen time.
2. Touch Content and Privacy Restrictions.
3. Tap Allowed apps and make sure AirDrop is turned on.

How to Use Airdrop to Send Items to Other Device

With AirDrop, you can quickly and efficiently transfer files across your friend's apple device. If you can't find your friend as a nearby AirDrop user, tell them to open Control Center and allow AirDrop to receive files. Here is how to go about it:

Open "Control Center." Turn Bluetooth and Wi-Fi on. Next, enable AirDrop and select either "Contacts Only" or "Everyone." Everyone is much easier to use.

To AirDrop photos, head to the Photos app and mark the photos, tap the "Share button," then choose "AirDrop" and select the target device. Next, tap "Accept" to receive the file.

To AirDrop contacts, head to the Contacts app, mark the contact, tap "Share Contact," and then select the target device. Tap "Accept" on the target device to receive the contact. You can only send one contact at a time which can be stressful sometimes.

Chapter 26: Add a Widget to Display the Battery Level as a Percentage

How to Add Widgets to Home Screen

Widgets can sit alongside your favorite apps on your home screen. And what's more, widgets now come in small, medium, and large sizes.

How to Add a Widget to Your Home Screen from the Today View

1. Open "Today view" by swiping right on your Home screen.
2. Hold down the widget you want to move. Drag to move the widget to your Home screen.

How to Add a New Widget

1. Hold down anywhere on your Home screen until the apps begin to jiggle.
2. Tap the + (plus) sign.
3. Tap on any of the pre-defined widgets or tap on an app's widget.
4. Swipe either left or right on the widget sizes to choose the size you want.
5. Tap and drag the widget you chose to a position on the Home screen. Tap "Done"

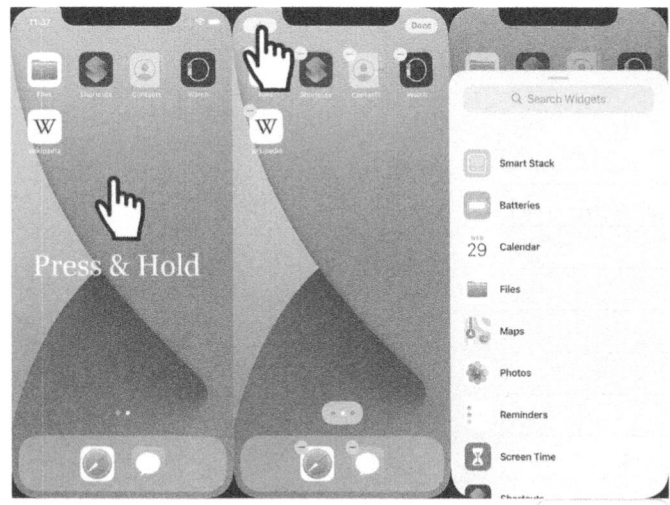

How to Edit a Widget

1. Hold down on a widget or Smart Stack until the context menu shows up.
2. Tap on "Edit Widget." If you're editing a single widget in a Smart Stack, you tap Edit "[Widget name]."
3. Use the options to tune the widget the way you want. Each widget has several options.

How to Add a Widget to the Today View

1. Open the "Today view." Hold down your screen until the apps begin to jiggle.
2. Tap on the + (plus) button and tap on the app's widget you want to move.
3. Swipe either left or right on the widget sizes to choose the size you want. Tap and drag the widget to the Today view.
4. To exit, tap Done.

How to Remove Widgets from the Home Screen

1. Hold down the widget until the context menu appears.
2. Tap on Remove Widget. Tap Remove.

Chapter 27: Make Your Own Memoji

Animoji is cool, but they have been taken to the next level by Memoji. You may already have a Memoji created if you up-grade from an iPhone X or iPhone 11. If your first iPhone with a TrueDepth front camera system is the  iPhone 12, it's your first chance to create your cartoon avatar.

Start by opening the Messages app, then by specifying a new post, or by opening an existing thread. Tap the Animoji icon at the right, then, at the beginning of the Animoji list, tap the + symbol.

Setting Up Your Memoji

The TrueDepth camera on your iPhone 12 comes with the Animoji feature first introduced far back as iOS 12.

1. Open the messages app and then open an existing message thread or start a new one.
2. Click the Animoji app in the bar along the bottom of the mes-sages screen. The icon shows a monkey.
3. Tap the '+' sign at the beginning of the list of Animoji.
4. Start tweaking your memoji; you have several options in skin color, hairstyle, head shape etc.
5. When you are satisfied, tap done in the upper right corner. You should see your new memoji among the Animoji picker.

Apple continues to push the memoji character creation, making it more diverse and expressive. There are several new hairstyles with the updated memoji, including man bun, top knot, etc.

iOS 14 also boasts some cool new updates to your favorite memojis.

- There are fresh hairstyles, headwear options, face coverings, and more age options to better express your personality.
- There are three new emoji stickers: a hug, a fist bump, and a blush.
- Memoji and emoji stickers now look even more expressive thanks to revamped facial and muscle structures.
- There are 16 new head wears and 16 new hairstyles.
- There are also new face coverings. You can add face coverings and change the masks' color, which seems relevant in these coronavirus pandemic times.

How to Use Them

Apple's Animojis are widely-used custom, animated 3D avatars that map your face and allow you to overlay your voice through the emoji. These animoji could be a Fox, a Dog, a Lion, an Owl, a zebra, etc. The feature makes use of facial recognition technology to generate three-dimensional emojis that mimic your facial movements and expressions.

To access animojis and memojis, tap on the app icon between the camera and the text box. Once open, you'll see different icons for GIFs, apps, animoji, digital touch, music, and YouTube. These icons give you access to these other features.

For the animoji feature, once you tap on it to open, it begins mapping your face and tracking all your facial movements. And if you tap on the record button (which is a red button at the right edge midway of the display), you can record the facial movements and sound projection and then send the recording to a contact when you're done recording. There are all kinds of different animojis that you can get access to and use for animation.

Chapter 28: Set Up Emergency Medical ID and Health Records

Setting Up Your Medical ID

Some features on your iPhone 12 are for fun, some for convenience but this can literally save your life.

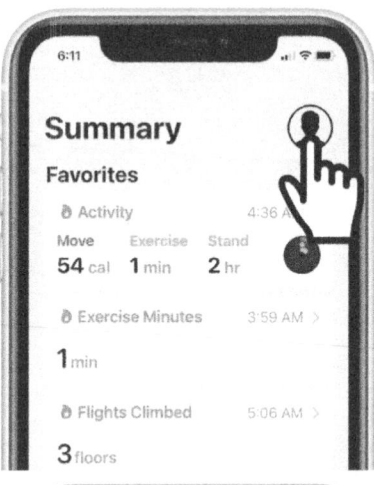

1. Open the health app
2. Tap on your profile picture at the upper right
3. Tap Medical ID
4. Tap edit in the upper right
5. Fill out your details
6. Tap Done.

Download Health Records in Health on iPhone

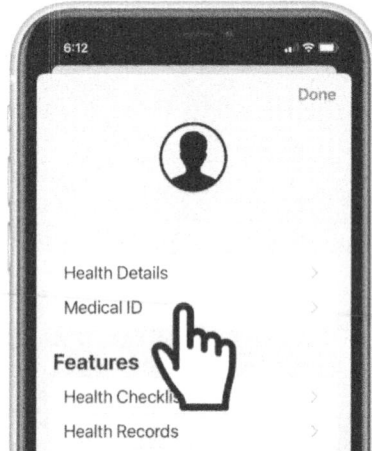

The Health app provides access to information from supported health organizations about your allergies, conditions, medications, and mo countries or regions).

Note: Your health organization may not appear in tions are added regularly.

The Health Records Screen in the Health Applicati

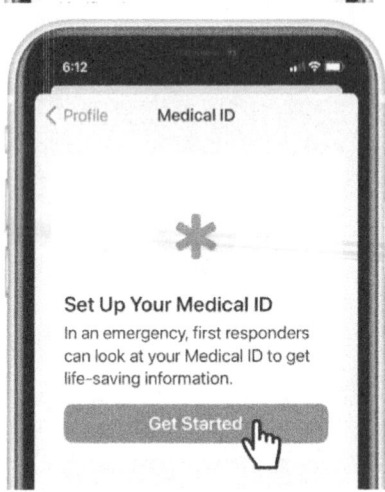

The screen displays categories including

signs, and conditions. Below the list of categories is a button for Widell Medical. The Browse button is selected at the bottom of the screen.

When iPhone is locked with a passcode, Touch ID, or Face ID, all health data in the Health app, in addition to what you add to your Medical ID, is encrypted.

Set Up Automatic Downloads

1. Touch your profile photo or initials at the top right. In the event, you don't see your profile photo or initials, touch Summary or Browse at the base of the screen, and then slide to the top of the screen.
2. Touch Medical Records and do one of the following:
   - Arrange your first download, tap Get
   - Arrange downloads for further accounts, tap Add account.
3. Enter the name of an organization, such as a clinic or hospital, where you get your medical records. Or enter the name of the city or state where you live to find a list of nearby organizations.
4. Touch a result to open it.
5. Under Available to connect, touch the Connect to Account button to go to the login screen of your patient portal.
6. Enter the username and password you use for that organization's patient web portal and follow the instructions on the screen.

View Your Medical Records

Touch Browse in the lower right to display the Health Categories screen and do one of the following:

- Touch the search field, and then enter the name of a health record category (such as Clinical Vitals) or a type of information (such as blood pressure).

- Scroll down and touch a category (such as Allergies or Clinical Vital Signs) in Medical Records.
- Scroll down and tap on the name of a specific organization.

Adjust Medical Record Notification Settings

Go to Settings> Notifications> Health and then choose options.

Erase an Organization and Its Records from iPhone

1. At the top right, tap your profile picture or initials and then tap Medical records.
2. Touch an organization name, then touch Remove account.

Share Your Logs with Other Applications

Third-party applications may request access to your medical records. Before granting access, be sure to trust the app with your data.

1. To grant access, choose which categories to share, such as allergies, medications, or immunizations, when prompted.
2. Choose whether you want to access your current and future medical records or just your current records. If you choose to share only your current records, you will be asked to grant access when new records are downloaded to your iPhone.
3. To stop sharing medical records with the app, turn off the permission to read health data.

Make and Allocate Your Medical ID in Health on iPhone

In the Health application, you can make an Emergency Medical ID that contains data about your ailments, hypersensitivities, meds, and then some. First responders and others can view this critical information right on their iPhone, even when it's locked.

At the point when you add emergency contacts to your clinical ID, they are consequently advised when you use Emergency SOS from your iPhone or when utilized from your Apple Watch.

You can also allow your medical identification information to be automatically sent to emergency services, through a secure third-party service, when you call, text, or use emergency SOS from your iPhone or Apple Watch (only on the USA; watchOS 6.2. 5 or higher) if Apple Watch is connected to a Wi-Fi or cellular network without your iPhone nearby; (texting 911 is not available everywhere).

Create Changes to Your Medical ID

1. Touch your profile photo or initials at the top right. In the event, you don't see your profile photo or initials, click Summary or Browse at the base of the screen, and then scroll to the upper part of the screen.
2. Touch Medical ID and do one of the following:
   - Create a Medical ID: Tap Get Started.
   - Change your medical ID: Touch Edit.

Important: To automatically send your medical identification information to emergency services when you call or text 911 or use Emergency SOS, activate Emergency Sharing (the US only; SMS to emergency numbers not available in all locations). Tap More info to learn how Apple protects your privacy.

To allow emergency services and others to see your medical ID when your iPhone is locked, Show, when locked, is on by default. Do not disable this option unless you want to prevent emergency services from seeing your medical ID.

A medical ID screen. At the bottom are the options to display your medical identification information when the iPhone screen is locked and when you make an emergency call.

A first responder views their Medical ID from the lock screen by swiping up or pressing the Home button (depending on the iPhone model), tapping Emergency on the password screen, and then tapping Medical ID.

Tip: You can rapidly see your Medical ID from the Home screen; long-press the Health application symbol, at that point, select Medical ID.

Control Health Functions with the Health Menu or Checklist on iPhone

Use the Health Checklist to view and activate important functions in the Health app.

1. In the top right, tap your profile picture or your initials.
2. In the event, you don't see your profile picture or initials tap Summary or better still explore or Browse at the bottom of the screen, then slide to the top of the screen.
3. Touch Health Menu or Checklist.

4. Tap to activate an item in the list or get more information about it.
5. When finished, touch Done.

Backup Your Health Data On iPhone

When you sign in with your Apple ID, your health and fitness information in the Health app is automatically saved to iCloud. Your information is encrypted while it is being sent between iCloud and your device and while it is stored in iCloud.

Furthermore, in utilizing iCloud, or if you are not using iCloud, you can reinforce your health data by encrypting a computer backup.

Stop Storing Your Health Data In iCloud

Proceed to Settings. Then, input [your name]> iCloud and deactivate Health.

Using the Health App to Set Up Sleep Schedules

1. To set up a sleep schedule, tap Browse at the bottom right and tap Sleep
2. Next, swipe up and tap Get Started just under Set Up Sleep
3. Follow the directions
4. Making Changes to your next Alarm
5. From bottom right, tap Browse and tap Sleep
6. Navigate down to your time table and tap Edit
7. To make changes to your time table for go-

167

ing to bed and waking up, select alarm options and tap Done when you finish.

Changing or Adding a Sleep Schedule

1. From bottom right, tap Browse and tap Sleep
2. Next, Navigate down to your Schedule. Tap full schedule & options
3. Tap Edit to change a sleep schedule
4. To add a sleep schedule, tap Add Schedule for Other Days.

If you want to switch off all sleep schedules, from bottom right, tap Browse, tap Sleep, tap Full Schedule & Options. Turn off Sleep Schedule at screen top.

Changing Your Wind Down Schedule and Activity

Wind down activities like reading or playing music appear on the lock screen if sleep mode is in effect

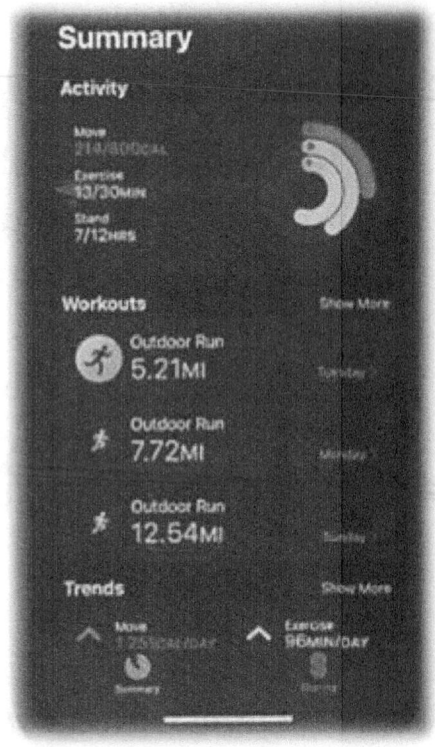

1. From bottom right, tap Browse, tap Sleep, tap Full Schedule & Options
2. To change when to activate sleep mode, tap Wind Down and choose a time
3. Tap Wind Down Short cuts to add or remove an activity.

Chapter 29: How You Can Find Your Lost iPhone

Find My App could not be active without being initially activated through the Settings App. Therefore, for you to make the feature of Find My App to be functional do the following steps:

- **Find Friends and Family Members or**
- **Share your location with others**

Set Up Find My

How You Can Activate Find My on Your iPhone

Hint: "Find My" is automatically turned on when you Sign In to your new iPhone with your Apple ID, but, there is a need for you to find out if Find My iPhone, Enable Offline Finding and Send Last Location are activated.

1. **Homescreen: Hit on Settings**
2. **Hit on your Name/Sign in to Your iPhone beside the profile picture.**
3. **Apple ID: Hit on Find My**
4. **Hit on Find My iPhone to select "On" if the activation feature is Off.**

Find My iPhone

Turn On the activators of the following if they are Off:

- **Find My iPhone: It will always request your Password to locate, erase, or lock your iPhone.**

- **Enable Offline Finding:** Your iPhone will be located even when it is not connected to a cellular or Wi-Fi network.
- **Send Last Location:** iCloud will automatically send the location of your iPhone to Apple when the battery is drastically low.
- Hit on My Location to select This Device.
- Hit on Share My Location's Activator to put On the switch.

What to Do After You Have Lost Your iPhone

There is a possibility of misplacing your iPhone in a location that you could not recollect because you had visited more than three places before you could remember that your iPhone is missing or it was stolen by a thief.

Also, you might have kept the iPhone in a compartment that is best known to you only but after a while, you could not remember specifically where exactly you had hidden the iPhone.

However, Apple has made a reliable way of locating your iPhone with the use of Find My iPhone and iCloud Map Detection or Google Map to specifically describe and identify the location of your iPhone wherever it had been kept.

First Finding Solution

On Mac or PC:

1. Use any of the available browsers such as Chrome, Mozilla Firefox, Internet Explorer, Safari, Opera, Lynx, or Konqueror.
2. In the Web Add text field type icloud.com.
3. iCloud Homepage: Sign In with your Apple ID which includes your Email and Password.
4. Click on Find iPhone Icon among the icons on the screen.

5. **iCloud Find My iPhone: Location Map will display on the screen.**

6. **At the top bar center of the screen click on All Devices.**

7. **On the drop-down, select your iPhone. (If you are using more than one Apple device that is using the same Apple ID. You will see all the Apple devices on the drop-down.)**

8. **The Map will zoom out to indicate the iPhone location with a black circle and your iPhone' Name label.**

9. **At the right corner, you will see 3 options you can use to help your findings: Play Sound, Lost Mode, and Erase iPhone.**

   - **Play Sound: If you pretty sure that the iPhone is around (home, workshop, or office) then you can click Play Sound immediately you will start hearing vibration with sound. The sound will continue until you hit on Find My iPhone Alert OK.**

   - **Lost Mode: This option perfect when you discovered that you can no longer recover/find your iPhone again then you can click on Lost Mode.**

       A. **Phone Number Dialog Box: Type your Phone Number (that can be called by the finder) and click on Next at the top right corner of the dialog box.**

       B. **Click on the Text box, type the message that will be shown on your iPhone 12 screen. e.g. "Please I have lost this iPhone. Kindly Call Me. Thank you" and click on Done at the top right angle of the dialog box. Automatically the iPhone will be locked. It will only be unlocked if you enter your passcode or through your Face ID.**

   - **Erase iPhone: This option is accurate when you realized that the iPhone could not be located, then, click Erase iPhone to completely remove all your vital and confidential data, applications (apps) & documents from the iPhone quickly.**

Second Finding Solution

This is can be used when you are having Google Map App on your iPhone but if do not have the app you can use the iCloud method above.

On Mac or PC:

1. Use any of the available browsers such as Chrome, Mozilla Firefox, Internet Explorer, Safari, Opera, Lynx, or Konqueror.
2. In the Web Add text field type www.google.com/maps
3. Google Maps: Click on Menu Icon at the top left side of the Search Google Maps Text Field.
4. Menu: Select Your Timeline (Timeline will show various locations you have been with your iPhone on Google maps with an indication of red color).
5. At the left side of the screen click on Today at the front of the Timeline.
6. Immediately a line will displace your different movement today on Google maps to know where your iPhone could be found.
7. You can zoom in on the map to make the location to be closer and clearer for you to see the location very well.
8. You can increase the displacement line (appear in blue) at the left side of the screen to see more of different places with their specific time in hours, minutes, and seconds that you moved from a particular place to another place till the final place where the iPhone could be found.

Note: You won't see the exact spot where the iPhone could be found on the Google map but you could only know the environment where you can see the iPhone.

How You Can Use Another iPhone to Track Your Lost iPhone

The method of tracking your lost iPhone on the computer is virtually the same as the method and processes of locating your lost iPhone on another iPhone.

If you are having two iPhones in your family or your friend is have one, you can easily use the available iPhone to quickly discover where your iPhone is kept or the location at which it could be found with either hope of recovery or not.

1. Homescreen: Hit on Find My App Icon
2. Find My: Hit on the Devices icon at the bottom center of your iPhone.
3. Devices: Hit on your lost iPhone 12's Name (e.g. Ephong's iPhone) that is your first name will be used to qualified the lost iPhone.
4. iPhone 12's Name: Swipe up from the top edge center of the page to select one of the available options below:
   - Play Sound: Having 100% assurance of finding it.
   - Directions: If it is discovered on the map and you want it to be tracked down.
   - Notifications: You will be notified when the iPhone is found.
   - Mark as Lost: If the recovery chances of your iPhone is 70–80% but the location on the map displayed is extremely far. Then you can hit on Active.
   - Erase This Device: If the chance of recovering your iPhone is less than 50% which is very narrow, then you can choose the option by tapping it.

Hint: if you eventually selected Erase This Device because you have initially lost hope of finding it, as a result, you would not be able to track your iPhone again. But, if by slim opportunity you found the iPhone, you will only be able to restore all the erased data and documents on your iPhone through iCloud backup.

How You Can Share Your Location with Others

You will need to select the people that you wanted to share your location with. This option will enable you to track down your lost iPhone on your friend's iPhone.

1. Homescreen: Hit on Find My App Icon
2. Find My: Hit on the People icon at the bottom left of the screen.
3. People: Hit on Start Sharing Location Start Sharing Location
4. Type the Name of the Person you want to share your location into the Text Field and hit on Send at the top right angle of the page.
5. An Optional Dialog Box will show up to select "time for the sharing of your location with the person." Select any of the flowing options: Share for One Hour, Share Until End of Day or Share Indefinitely
6. Notification: On a Dialog box you will see "You Shared Your Location with the Person's Contact. Hit on OK.

How to Use Your iPhone IMEI Code to Block Your Lost iPhone

Your iPhone IMEI Code is very important to you when your iPhone has been confirmed lost and no hope of recovery.

It is very essential to know your iPhone IMEI code that serves as the main personal Apple device identification.

You could use your IMEI code to confirm if your iPhone is originally manufactured by Apple Company or being produced by a fake manufacturer. It can also be used to unlock your iPhone.

Therefore, you have to take the following wise step to confirm your iPhone IMEI code:

1. Homescreen: Hit on the Phone App.
2. Phone Page: Dial Asterisk "", Hash "#", Zero "0", Six "6", Asterisk "", Hash "#" (i.e. #06#) on Keypad.
3. Tap on the Call button.
4. Immediately, the IMEI code will appear on your iPhone screen.
5. Keep the IMEI Code in a confidential planner.
6. Call your Phone Operator, report the lost iPhone, and dictate your iPhone IMEI code for the lost iPhone to be blocked.

Conclusion

The iPhone 12 and 12 mini, are perfect for anyone who doesn't need the Pro camera features. Remember that hot fashion item everyone was dying to have in the past, but soon became unfashionable, and then became stylish yet again? Well, the same thing applies to the new iPhone 12 lineup of devices launched recently by Apple.

Say goodbye to those curved edges we've all associated iPhone's flagship line with lately, and say hello to a sharper, rectangular design that Apple hopes will stir up some of the nostalgia linked with the old days of the iPhone 4. To Apple's credit, that design was hailed as one of the best smartphone designs ever.

The shield covering the display of all iPhone 12 series devices, which Apple claims is made from ceramic, is durable enough to withstand falls from considerable heights. The close-fitting borders provide room for an even larger ultra-high-definition display.

5G is set to change the world with profoundly faster Internet speeds, and Apple doesn't want to be left out. The iPhone 12's hardware and the iOS 14 operating system have been optimized to provide a seamless 5G experience.

The A14 Bionic chipset that powers all the devices in the iPhone 12 series has a smaller five-nanometer transistor, which makes it smaller and more energy-efficient while retaining class-leading processing power.

A new and enhanced camera unit makes the 12 lineup of devices even better at photography. The larger iPhone 12 Pro Max takes these advances up a notch. Its larger sensor significantly increases the details captured in every photo or video recording and helps enhance low light performance almost twice that of the iPhone 11 Pro Max.

The iPhone 12, iPhone 12 Pro, and iPhone 12 Pro Max all possess state-of-the-art video recording capabilities. Apple's latest flagship offering further narrows the gulf between professional high definition cameras and smartphone cameras. It can capture, replay, and edit 10-bit High Dynamic Range (HDR) recording with the help of Dolby Vision technology.

I'm sure all this information was helpful to you, and you will take 5 minutes to write a review of my long work!

Enjoy your iPhone 12.